Editor
Melissa Romero, M.F.A.

Managing Editor
Ina Massler Levin, M.A.

Editor-in-Chief
Sharon Coan, M.S. Ed.

Illustrator
Ken Tunell

Cover Artist
Barb Lorseyedi

Art Coordinator
Denice Adorno

Imaging
Alfred Lau
Temo Parra

Product Manager
Phil Garcia

Publisher
Mary D. Smith, M.S. Ed.

Practice and Learn
the
ALPHABET

Author

Marie Cecchini

Teacher Created Resources, Inc.
6421 Industry Way
Westminster, CA 92683
www.teachercreated.com
ISBN: 978-0-7439-3616-3

©2001 Teacher Created Resources, Inc.
Reprinted, 2007
Made in U.S.A.

Table of Contents

Introduction

The formation and use of letters are abstract concepts to young children. To make letters a more concrete concept, we need to teach them through the use of familiar objects, manipulatives, games, and art activities. As children work with letters using these kinds of materials and activities, they begin to understand the connection between letters and sounds.

The activities in the first section of this book incorporate letters within various areas of the curriculum. Most of the activities will work with more than one letter. It is best to introduce one letter at a time and include the letter sound along with the letter name. Choose activities from those suggested that best suit your program sequence.

The second section introduces children to color names. The children color, cut, and glue shape projects to construction paper, reinforcing initial consonant sounds and fine motor skills. The children will also play detective as they search for specific letters, helping them to develop visual discrimination skills and reinforcing letter name recognition. This section will also provide children with the opportunity to learn to write the letter forms. They will trace the form of each letter with their fingers and pencils, then practice writing the letters.

The third section provides you, the teacher, with a number of games and activities using all of the letters in the alphabet. These activities will allow children to practice naming letters, forming their sounds, and reading color words.

The fourth section contains material you may wish to share with the parents of your children as the class works its way through the alphabet.

A bibliography of alphabet resources appears at the end of the book. You may wish to make use of it throughout your program.

Introduction *(cont.)*

The activities in this book are designed to do the following:

1. Develop fine motor skills.
2. Develop visual perception.
3. Introduce and reinforce letter names.
4. Help the children learn to differentiate between upper and lower case letters.
5. Help the children learn to associate letters with their sounds.
6. Introduce color names.
7. Practice letter formation.

These general materials are needed to complete the exercises included in this book:

- crayons and/or markers
- scissors
- pencils
- construction paper
- yarn
- glue

Specific curriculum areas require additional materials as listed per project.

Alphabet Science

Body of Letters

Materials: chart paper, markers, magazines, glue

Directions:

1. Have the children watch as you write the upper- and lowercase forms of a letter at the top of a sheet of chart paper. Explain how the letters are written as you draw them. Invite the students to name the letter and say the sound it represents.

2. Challenge the children to name and point to various parts of their bodies that begin with the same sound. An example would be foot, face, and finger for **F**. Write the names of the body parts that the children contribute on the chart paper.

3. During independent time, encourage the children to find pictures of these body parts in old magazines, cut the pictures out, and glue them to the chart paper next to the appropriate word.

Letter Street

Materials: shoe box lid, marker, paper clips, magnets

Directions:

1. Draw and color a block letter shape inside the shoe box lid. Tell the children, "This is H, L, M, etc. Street."

2. Place a paper clip in the shoebox lid. Tell the children, "This is a pretend car." Demonstrate for the students how to move the magnet beneath the lid to move the paper clip car.

3. Help individual children to hold the lid steady as they use the magnet to steer the paper clip car over the letter shape.

   Safety Note: Activities using small objects, such as paper clips, need to be closely supervised.

Magnet Letters

Materials: letter cards, paper clips, magnets

Directions:

1. Have the children use the magnets to pull paper clips onto the cards in the shape of the letter. Disengage each paper clip by holding it in place with a finger as the magnet is removed.

   Safety Note: Activities using small objects, such as paper clips, need to be closely supervised.

Alphabet Science *(cont.)*

Rainbow Letters

Materials: chalkboard easel, colored chalk, chalkboard eraser

Directions:

1. Draw a seven-arc rainbow shape, one arc for each color (red, orange, yellow, green, blue, indigo, violet). As you draw, tell the children what you are making. Name the colors, and introduce the word "arc." Label each arc with the first letter of its color name. Have the children say the letters and their sounds.

2. Invite individual children to come to the board. Have each child choose a chalk, name the color, say its letter, then write the letter in the appropriate arc.

3. Keep the board, chalk, and eraser available for the children to practice letters on their own during independent time.

Seed Letters

Materials: construction paper, markers, glue, seeds

Directions:

1. Have the children write a specific letter shape on a sheet of construction paper, then trace this letter with glue.

2. Provide the children with corresponding flower or vegetable seeds to press into the glue letter. For example, use sunflower seeds for **S**, watermelon seeds for **W**, etc.

   Safety Note: Activities using small objects, such as seeds, need close supervision.

Scented Letter Fans

Materials: index cards, pencils, glue, fruit flavored gelatin powder, craft sticks, tape

Directions:

1. Have the children use pencil to write a specific letter form on an index card, then trace their letters with glue.

2. Provide the children with corresponding fruit flavored gelatin powder to sprinkle over the glue, such as orange for **O**, lime for **L**, etc. Shake off excess powder.

3. Allow the glue to dry, then tape a craft stick handle to the back of each card. As the students fan themselves, they will smell the scent of their letters.

   Safety Note: Remind the children that this is a project and the gelatin is not to be eaten. Prepare additional gelatin to serve as a snack, if you wish.

Alphabet Science *(cont.)*

Letter Garden

Materials: foam meat trays, soil, grass seed, water

Teacher Preparation: Do this project outside or on a newspaper covered table.

Directions:

1. Have the children place soil in their trays, smooth the surface of the soil, then use an index finger to draw a letter shape on the surface of the soil.
2. Let the students sprinkle grass seed into their letter lines, then smooth the surface of the soil to cover the seeds.
3. Keep the gardens moist, and after a few days, the letters will begin to grow.

Shadow Letters

Materials: a desk lamp or flashlight, a darkened area of the classroom

Directions:

1. Shine the light on the wall in a darkened area of the classroom.
2. Invite individual students to use their bodies, fingers, and hands to create shadow letters on the wall.

Rainy Day Letters

Materials: water-soluble markers, white construction paper, a rainy day or water-filled spray bottles

Directions:

1. Have the children draw a letter shape on white paper using one of the following color pairs: red and blue, blue and yellow, yellow and red.
2. Set the drawings out in a light rain shower for a few seconds.
3. Return the drawings to the classroom and have the children observe the results of the color blending.

Variation: In absence of a rainy day, simulate a rain shower using a water-filled spray bottle. Spray lightly.

Night Sky

Materials: dark blue construction paper, star shaped stickers

Directions:

1. Let the children place the stickers on the paper to create their own letter constellations.

Alphabet Science *(cont.)*

Constellations

Materials: black construction paper, chalk or white crayons, pieces of corrugated cardboard such as sides from a box, blunt needles or pencils, flashlight, darkened classroom

Directions:

1. Have the children use chalk or white crayon to write a letter shape on black paper.

2. Place the papers on corrugated cardboard and let the children use blunt needles or pencil points to poke holes along their letter lines.

3. Let the children take turns shining the flashlight through the holes in their papers onto the ceiling to create letter star formations.

   Safety Note: Even with blunt needles, this project requires direct supervision.

Colors in Black

Materials: coffee filters, water-soluble black markers, spray bottles of water, baking racks

Directions:

1. Have the children draw a black letter shape onto a flattened coffee filter, then place the filter onto the baking rack.

2. Let the children spray a little water (spray lightly, do not soak) over their letters.

3. Observe and name the various colors that filter out from the black.

Weather Word Stamp Letters

Materials: weather picture stamps, washable ink stamp pads, construction paper

Directions:

1. Let the children use individual stamps to shape specific letters on construction paper. For example, use a sun stamp to write an **S**, an umbrella stamp to write a **U**, etc.

Alphabet Math

Bulletin Board Name Graph

Materials: butcher or craft paper, yarn or ribbon, markers, construction paper, stapler, staples

Teacher Preparation: Back your chalkboard with one long sheet of craft or butcher paper. Determine which letters of the alphabet are used as first letters in students' names. Staple ribbon or yarn to make a column for each of these letters on your bulletin board. Use marker to write a letter at the top of each column.

Directions:

1. Have the children draw self-portraits on separate sheets of construction paper and write their names below their drawings.

2. Help the students place their self-portraits in the correct columns. For example, all pictures of children whose names begin with **T** will hang in the **T** column.

3. Challenge the children to tell you which letter begins the most and least number of names.

Search and Count

Materials: chart paper, marker

Directions:

1. Invite the children to search the room and find places where words and letters are used, such as the center signs, the calendar, weather chart, and exit signs.

2. List the names of the places they find.

3. Count the number of places where letters were used.

Tic-Tac-Toe

Materials: cardboard or poster board, markers, commercially produced plastic or rubber letters

Teacher Preparation: Cut several squares of cardboard or poster board. Draw lines on each square to make tic-tac-toe boards.

Directions:

1. Have pairs of children use the boards with the letters to play tic-tac-toe with a twist. Instead of playing with X's and O's, have each pair of players use other letters of the alphabet, such as A's and B's, G's and Q's, etc.

2. The winner of each round is still the player who ends up with three letter markers in a row.

Alphabet Math *(cont.)*

Letter Patterns

Materials: strips of paper or poster board, markers, commercially prepared letter shapes or letter cards

Teacher Preparation: Use a marker to prepare letter pattern strips. You can use all upper case (**TT KK**), all lower case (**aa bb aa**), or combine the two (**SSS sss SSS**).

Directions:

1. Challenge the students to copy and/or complete each pattern using letter shapes or letter cards.

Size and Sound

Materials: familiar objects or pictures of familiar objects, such as a hat, pen, or book

Directions:

1. Display an object or picture of an object. Have the children identify the name of the object and the sound of the letter that begins that name.

2. Challenge the children to find and name other objects around the classroom that begin with the same sound but are smaller or larger than the first object.

Letter Count

Materials: magnetic or felt letters and numbers with the appropriate display board

Directions:

1. Place a letter and a number at the top of the board. Have the children name what is displayed, such as two A's or five D's.

2. Invite individual students to place the correct amount of that same letter on the board below the "instructions." For the above examples, the child would place two A's or five D's on the board.

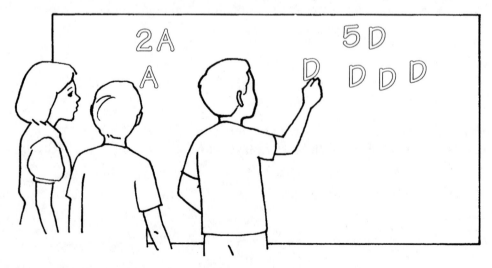

Alphabet Math *(cont.)*

Ordinal Counting

Materials: classroom wall alphabet strip, individual alphabet letter cards

Directions:

1. Have the children help arrange a small group of letter cards in alphabetical order. Show them how they can use the classroom wall alphabet strip or the alphabet song to help them remember the letter sequence.

2. Demonstrate for the students how to identify the placement of each letter in your group of cards as first, second, third, etc., then collect the cards and pass them out to individual children.

3. Challenge the card-holding children to arrange themselves in alphabetical order. Have them hold their cards for the class to see.

4. Have the class say the name of each person and the name of each letter that is first, second, etc. Encourage them to say the letter sounds in the same order.

Hide the Star

Materials: alphabet letter cards, a paper star cutout

Directions:

1. Choose 10 alphabet cards at random. Arrange them in a row on the floor or on a tabletop.

2. Work with the children to name the letters, their sounds, and their positions (first, second, etc.), in order from left to right.

3. Tell the students to cover their eyes while you hide the star cutout under one of the letter cards.

4. Challenge individual students to guess the name, sound, and position of the letter under which the star is hidden. The child who guesses correctly is the one who hides the star for the next round.

Sticks and Curves

Materials: commercially produced plastic letters, craft sticks

Directions:

1. Invite children to sort the letters into those made with only sticks (straight lines) and those made of sticks and curves (straight and curved lines), creating two piles.

2. Let each student choose and name a letter made of only sticks. Challenge the children to use the craft sticks to make the letters they have chosen.

Alphabet Math *(cont.)*

Name Numbers

Materials: paper, markers

Directions:

1. Have the children write their names on individual pieces of paper. Count the number of letters they used, and write this number on the paper.

2. Let the children hold their name papers as you work together to sort them into small groups whose names have the same number of letters. Discuss whose names have the most or least number of letters. How many names have the same number of letters?

3. Tell the children to check their names for letters that are used more than once. Have them underline these letters. Ask students to name the letter(s) they use more than once to spell their names.

Letter Box

Materials: cardboard box, wrapping paper, construction paper, marker, scissors, cellophane tape

Teacher Preparation: Remove the top from a cardboard box. Cover the box with wrapping paper. Draw and cut a block letter shape from construction paper to tape to one side of the box. To change letters, remove the first before replacing.

Directions:

1. Display the box. Talk with the children about the name and sound of the letter on the box.

2. Set the box in a special place for a few days. Encourage the children to search the classroom and their homes for items to place in the box that begin with the sound of the letter on the box. Stress the fact that they must get their parents' permission to bring in objects from home.

3. After several days, review the name and sound of the letter, then name each of the objects in the box. How many items were collected?

Number Names

Materials: number name cards (pages 187–190) and small objects such as craft sticks, cotton balls, or plastic game pieces

Teacher Preparation: Copy the numeral and word cards and laminate, if you wish. Cut the cards apart.

Directions:

1. Use the cards with groups of small objects to explore the idea that the numerals, words, and sets of objects have the same meaning.

Alphabet Language

Lace Letters

Materials: foam meat trays or paper plates, large tapestry needle (adult use), long shoelaces

Teacher Preparation: Use the needle to poke holes, creating letter shapes, in the foam meat trays or paper plates.

Directions:

1. Have the children lace the letter shapes with long shoelaces.

Letter Pairs

Materials: Mitten Match Cards (pages 168–180), markers, scissors, a small basket to store the mittens, laminator (optional)

Teacher Preparation: Copy the Mitten Match Cards. Help the children color the mitten designs to match. Laminate the pages if desired. Cut out the mittens and place them in the basket.

Directions:

1. Display one pair of mittens. Prompt the children to tell what is the same about the pair (the design), then what is different (upper/lower case, left/right). How can we tell which mitten would be for your left/right hand? Have the children raise and shake first their left hands, then their right.
2. Show the children how all upper- and lowercase mitten patterns match. Place the mittens back in the basket.
3. Challenge the children to match the mitten pairs and name the letters.

Stamp-a-Letter

Materials: letter stamps, washable ink stamp pads, paper

Directions:

1. Let the children use specific letter stamps to stamp letter shapes on paper. For example, have them use a **T** stamp to make the shape of a **T**.

Letter Mascot

Materials: stuffed animal with cap and sweater to wear, upper- and lowercase felt letters, masking or cellophane tape

Directions:

1. Each time you work on a new letter, use small, rolled pieces of tape to attach the new lowercase letter to the mascot's cap and the new uppercase letter to its sweater.
2. Use the letter mascot as a puppet or special friend to help introduce each new letter to the class.

Alphabet Language *(cont.)*

In the News

Materials: old magazines, newspapers, construction paper, scissors, glue

Directions:

1. Encourage the children to look through newspapers and magazines for a specific letter, such as **S** or **M**. Larger letters like those found in headlines will be easier to work with.

2. Have the students count out the letters they find and glue them to a piece of construction paper.

3. Share the children's work with the class. Point out the various forms used to make the same letter (curves/lines).

4. Display the work or save it to compile into a book.

Poster Shapes

Materials: poster board, old magazines and catalogs, scissors, glue, yarn, paper punch

Teacher Preparation: Draw and cut a large letter shape from poster board. Punch two holes in the top of the letter. Thread and knot a length of yarn through the holes to make a hanger.

Directions:

1. Have the children search through magazines for pictures of items whose names begin with the sound of the poster letter shape. Cut these pictures out.

2. Let the children identify their pictures, the letter name, and its sound. Invite them to glue their pictures to the poster board letter shape.

3. Suspend the letter poster from the classroom ceiling.

You've Got Mail

Materials: small boxes, paper bags or paper plates, markers, glue, stapler, colorful paper scraps, pens and pencils, unused postal or holiday cards

Directions:

1. Invite the children to decorate boxes, bags, or paper plates with markers and colorful bits of paper to create their own mailboxes. Be sure they place their names on their mailboxes.

2. Designate one area of the room as a post office. Display the mailboxes, provide a writing table, and supply the table with pens, pencils, unused holiday cards with envelopes, and postal cards. Encourage the children to write illustrated notes to deposit into each other's mailboxes. Allow them to check their mail each morning.

Alphabet Language *(cont.)*

Name Game

Materials: plastic, magnetic, or felt letters with the appropriate display board

Directions:

1. Demonstrate to the children that letters must be placed in a special sequence in order to spell words. First, spell a child's name on the board using the letters. Have the children name the letters and notice the sequence. Now rearrange the letters and ask the child whose name was originally spelled whether this "word" still spells his/her name.

2. Place mixed up letters of another child's name on the board. Have the class study the letters. Whose name will these letters make? Invite the children to help rearrange the letters to spell the name correctly.

Same and Different

Materials: index cards, pen

Teacher Preparation: Use the cards to prepare lists of three or four words each. All of the words but one in each list should begin with the same sound. A list example might be *tool, tub, kite, tank.*

Directions:

1. Have the children listen carefully as you read a list of words. Repeat the reading as necessary.

2. Challenge the student to tell which word does not belong.

Lunch Box Letters

Materials: an old lunch box, index cards, marker, cellophane tape

Teacher Preparation: Use an index card with marker and tape to decorate the front of an old lunch box with a letter.

Directions:

1. Invite individual children to take the lunch box home for an evening and fill it with a few objects whose names begin with the letter on the front. Remind the children that they must get their parents' permission before bringing any object from home to class.

2. The following day, let the lunch box detective share the collected items with the class.

Alphabet Language *(cont.)*

Letter Match Lotto

Materials: Lotto Cards (pages 150–153), Letter Pocket Cards (page 149), buttons or milk jug lids for markers, paper lunch bag

Teacher Preparation: Copy the Lotto Cards and the Letter Pocket Cards. Laminate all five sheets. Cut the Letter Pocket Cards apart.

Directions:

1. This game is designed for four players at a time. Distribute a lotto grid to each player. Drop the lowercase letter cards into the bag. Place a supply of buttons or milk jug lid markers in the center of the group, so everyone can reach them.

2. Have the players take turns holding the top of the bag closed while shaking it, then opening the bag to choose and display a lowercase letter card. Players who have a matching uppercase letter on their cards will cover that letter with a button or jug lid. The winner of the round is the first player to cover all of the letters on his/her card.

Variation: Use these materials in the same manner to play tic-tac-toe. This time the winner of each round will be the player to score three letters in a horizontal, vertical, or diagonal row.

Letter Sound Mobile

Materials: paper towel tubes, yarn, three inch squares of paper, markers or crayons, magazines and catalogs, glue, scissors, cellophane tape

Teacher Preparation: Cut paper into squares, making four for each child.

Directions:

1. Let the children count out four paper squares each. Have them write a different letter on each square.

2. Now have the children search for and cut out magazine or catalog pictures that begin with the sound of each letter they have written on a square. Let them glue their pictures to the backs of the appropriate letters.

3. Use tape and yarn to help the children suspend their letter-picture squares from cardboard tubes. Slide a longer length of yarn through each tube. Knot the ends of this longer yarn together to make hangers for the mobiles.

Alphabet Language *(cont.)*

Garland Necklaces

Materials: letter beads, long shoelaces

Directions:

1. Help the children string beads onto long shoelaces to spell their names. Tie the ends of each shoelace into a bow to make necklaces. Putting children's mother's name on the necklaces instead would create nice holiday or Mother's Day gifts.

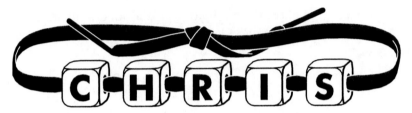

Variation: Prepare lettered, seasonal, paper cutouts to replace the beads. Punch two holes in each cutout. Have the children string the cutouts in alphabetical order by threading the laces into one hole and out from the other for each shape used. Use the garlands as classroom decorations.

Sound Textures

Materials: construction paper, markers, glue, various manipulatives depending on your chosen letter (cotton balls for **C**, toothpicks for **T**, paper clips for **P**, and sand for **S**)

Directions:

1. Have the children write a large letter shape on a sheet of construction paper. Trace these letter lines with glue.
2. Have the children set items that begin with the sound of that letter into the glue to form its shape.

Memory Match

Materials: commercially prepared upper-and lowercase letter cards, or write on index cards with marker to make your own

Directions:

1. Choose several pairs of letter cards, such as **C c**, **F f**, and **P p**. The number of pairs you use will depend upon the abilities of your group of children. Have the children name the letters and say their sounds.
2. Shuffle the cards, then place them facedown on a tabletop.
3. Let individual children take turns flipping over two cards each. If the players match an upper and lowercase letter, they keep the cards and get a second turn. If the cards do not match, the player turns them facedown again, and it is the next player's turn.
4. The game is over when all of the cards have been collected.

Alphabet Language *(cont.)*

Hide the Button

Materials: four colorful plastic cups, permanent marker, a button

Teacher Preparation: Turn the cups upside-down and print a different letter of the alphabet on each.

Directions:

1. Display the cups on the tabletop. Have the children name the letters printed on the cups. Turn the cups around so the children cannot see the letters.
2. Place a button under one of the cups, then slide the cups around to change their placement. Finish with the letter shapes facing the children. Challenge individual children to guess which letter the button is hiding under.
3. The child who finds the button is the next person to hide it and slide the cups.

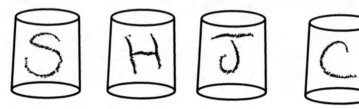

What's Missing?

Materials: plastic, magnetic, or felt letters with the appropriate display board

Directions:

1. Place letters on the board to spell the name of a child in the class, leaving out one of the letters.
2. Ask the children who they think this name belongs to.
3. Have the child named come to the board to add the missing letter.

Party Lights

Materials: Party Light Cut-Outs (pages 154–167), markers, laminator, length of ribbon or cord, two classroom chairs, clothespins, scissors

Teacher Preparation: Copy the Party Lights Cut-outs. Have the children help color them with marker, then laminate the pages. Cut out the lights.

Directions:

1. Suspend a length of ribbon or cord between two classroom chairs to make a pretend electrical cord. Use clothespins to hang the uppercase lights along the line, leaving a space between each.
2. Provide the children with additional clothespins and the lowercase lights. Challenge the children to hang the lowercase lights next to the appropriate capitals.

Variation: Print upper- and lowercase letters on clothespins. Place the lights and clothespins on a table. Have the children clip lowercase clothespins to uppercase lights and uppercase clothespins to lowercase lights.

Alphabet Movement

Hide and Seek Letters

Materials: commercially prepared plastic letters or letter cards, paper lunch bags

Teacher Preparation: Hide the letters in the classroom.

Directions:

1. Provide the students with lunch bags. Explain to them that the letters of the alphabet are hidden throughout the room, and it's their job to find letters to collect in their bags.

2. Give a signal to begin the search. Tell the children to come back to group when they can no longer find any letters.

3. Have the children display and name the letters they have found.

Letter Match

Materials: classroom chairs, marching band music, construction paper or index cards, marker, tape, craft sticks

Teacher Preparation: Print different letters of the alphabet on several sheets of paper or index cards. Tape one letter to each chair. Tape colorful paper triangles to craft sticks to make small pennant flags.

Directions:

1. Arrange the chairs in a row, facing alternate directions. Have the children form a "parade" line. Show the children how the seats alternate sides and that each chair is decorated with a letter.

2. Tell the children you are going to play marching music so they can march in a parade around the chairs. Explain that they must listen carefully because when you stop the music, they must sit in the nearest chair.

3. After the music stops, the children must name the letters on their chairs to stay in the game. Children eliminated from the game are given small pennant flags to wave while watching the parade.

Search and Seek Sounds

Materials: letter cards

Directions:

1. Display a letter card. Have the children name the letter and tell its sound. Let them search the room to find and choose one item whose name begins with the same sound. Have them bring their item back to the group.

2. Invite each child to show and name the found object. Have the class name the object and the letter sound.

Alphabet Movement *(cont.)*

Body Letters

Materials: paper bag, letter cards or shapes, an obstacle-free area of the classroom or playground

Directions:

1. Place the letter cards or shapes into the bag and shake to mix.
2. Let individual children draw one letter from the bag. Have each child make use of legs, arms, or fingers to make the shape of the letter drawn.
3. Challenge the class to name the letter, then display the letter card or shape.

Variation: Omit the letter shapes or cards. Encourage the children to use their bodies and their imaginations to shape letters they know. What letters can they make using their whole bodies? Invite children to work with partners to discover what letters can be shaped using more than one person.

Bean Bag Grid

Materials: large sheet of craft paper or tag board, marker, beanbags

Teacher Preparation: Draw a nine-square grid on the paper or tag board. Label each section of the grid with a different letter.

Directions:

1. Have the students take turns tossing one of three beanbags onto the grid. They get a point for naming each letter on which their beanbags land.

Variations:

1. Challenge the students to say the sounds of the letters on which their beanbags land.
2. Have the students work in pairs with two beanbag colors to play tic-tac-toss. The players must get three beanbags in a row and name these letters to win the round.

Sound Movements

Materials: paper, marker

Directions:

1. Invite the students to contribute suggestions for body movements whose names begin with a specific letter, such as wink, wiggle, walk, and wave for W, or bend, balance, bounce, and bump for B. List their contributions on paper, underlining the first consonant.
2. Review the action list created by the students, one by one. Challenge the children to demonstrate each movement as they repeat the letter sound. For example, repeat the B sound as they make a bouncing motion.

Alphabet Movement *(cont.)*

Letter Tape

Materials: obstacle-free area of the classroom, masking tape (preferably painter's masking tape as it will peel off easily later)

Teacher Preparation: Use the masking tape to construct a large letter form on the classroom floor.

Directions:

1. Have the children name the tape letter, then take turns "balancing" on the tape line as they walk around the letter shape.
2. Challenge the children to skip, hop, gallop, crawl, etc. around the letter shape.

Variation: Lay a clothesline letter shape out on the playground. Proceed in the same manner as above.

Hot Potato Soup

Materials: plastic, wooden, rubber, or cardboard letter shapes and music

Directions:

1. Have the children sit in a circle. Display a letter for the children to name. Explain that while they hear music playing, they are to pass the letter from person to person around the circle, but when the music stops, the letter also stops. When the music stops, the person holding the letter must identify it and say its sound to remain in the game. If the player cannot name the letter and say its sound, he or she goes into the "soup" (sits in the center of the circle).
2. As each letter's name and sound are identified, replace it with a new one.

Variation: Play Secret Hot Potato Soup by placing an unidentified letter into a paper bag before passing it around. When the music stops, the person holding the bag must open it to discover and name the secret letter. Place a different letter in the bag for each round.

Sign Letters

Materials: book on sign language from the school library

Directions:

1. Invite the children to join you in learning to sign the alphabet.
2. Assist individual students in learning to sign their names.

Alphabet Movement *(cont.)*

Letter Ring Toss

Materials: plastic container lids, empty cans or boxes, marker, clothespins, scissors

Teacher Preparation: Cut the centers from several plastic lids to create rings. Label each box or can with a different letter. Clip two to four clothespins onto the rim of each can or box, creating pegs.

Directions:

1. Let the children take turns tossing the plastic rings to try and encircle a clothespin peg. When the students ring a peg, they must name the letter on the box or can.

Catch-a-Letter

Materials: large rubber ball, permanent marker, music

Teacher Preparation: Use marker to draw letter shapes onto a large ball.

Directions:

1. Have a group of children stand in a circle and toss the ball back and forth to each other while music plays.
2. When the music stops, the player holding the ball must identify the name of the letter in front of him or her and say a word that begins with that letter.

Variation: Have the children sit on the floor in a circle and roll the ball to each other while you play music. When the music stops, proceed in the same manner as above.

Fishing Fun

Materials: several round metal lids from frozen juice cans, stickers, yardstick, yarn, a small magnet, permanent marker, scissors

Teacher Preparation: Write a letter on one side of each metal lid. Place a sticker on the back of each lid to match the sound of the letter, such as placing a sun sticker on the back of the **S**. Cut a length of yarn for fishing line. Tie one end of the yarn length to the end of the yardstick to make a fishing pole. Tie the opposite end of the yarn to a small magnet.

Directions:

1. Place the prepared lids on the floor. Invite individual students to "fish" for a letter. Have the children identify the letter name and sound for each fish-lid they "catch."

Variation: Invite the children to help write letters and attach stickers to the lids.

Alphabet Movement *(cont.)*

Bucket o'Letters

Materials: plastic dishpans or buckets, six beanbags, masking tape, two sets of alphabet letters or letter cards

Teacher Preparation: Place tape on the floor to create a standing line for tossing.

Directions:

1. Divide the class into two teams. Provide each team with a bucket and three beanbags.
2. Team members take turns tossing the beanbags toward their buckets. The team earns one alphabet letter for each beanbag that makes it into the bucket. The first team to earn the entire alphabet wins the game.

Alphabet Antics

Materials: letter cards, music, obstacle-free area of the classroom

Teacher Preparation: Place the letter cards on the floor in the shape of a circle.

Directions:

1. Invite the children to walk, hop, skip, and crawl around the letter circle while you play music. When the music stops, have the children name the letter nearest them.

Target Toss

Materials: several empty plastic soda bottles, squares of paper, marker, tape, table, a tennis or sponge ball

Teacher Preparation: Write a different letter on each paper square. Tape one paper square letter to each soda bottle. Line the bottles up on a tabletop.

Directions:

1. Let the children take turns tossing the ball at the bottles. They must name the letters on the bottles they knock down.

Around Town

Materials: a nice day, a camera, poster board, marker, glue, adult volunteers

Directions:

1. Take the students on an observational walk around the neighborhood. Prompt the children to point out any signs they see along the way. Photograph each sign the students notice. Talk about the letters on the signs.
2. Develop the film. Glue the pictures to a sheet of poster board. Ask the children to remember and name the places where they saw the signs. Have them name the first letter on each sign for you to write below the picture.

Alphabet Art

Name Sign

Materials: construction paper, markers, glitter, glue

Directions:

1. Help the children fold a sheet of construction paper in half. Let them write their names on one half of this paper.

2. Have the children trace their names with glue, then sprinkle glitter over the glue.

3. When the glue dries, their folded Name Sign can be used on a desk or dresser at home.

Silhouette Letters

Materials: newspaper, white construction paper, plastic or rubber alphabet letters, water, food color, spray bottles, bucket

Directions:

1. Fill several spray bottles with water. Tint each with a different food color. Place additional water in a bucket to rinse the plastic or rubber letters. Cover a tabletop with newspaper.

2. Have the children lay white paper onto the newspaper-covered surface. Let them arrange letters on their papers. Have them spray colored water over their letters.

3. Remove the letters and drop them into the bucket of water.

4. Silhouettes of the letters remain for the children to frame or use as a gift-wrap.

Sound Hat

Materials: construction paper, magazines, scissors, glue, stapler

Directions:

1. Prepare a hat-sized strip of paper for each child. Have the students draw and cut a paper letter shape to glue at the center of this strip, then cut magazine pictures to coordinate with this letter sound to glue along the strip. Staple finished hats to size.

Alphabet Art *(cont.)*

Sunny Day Letters

Materials: prepared colored glue (or make your own by mixing a few drops of food color into white glue), wax paper, dental floss

Directions:

1. Let the children use colored glue to draw a letter shape on a piece of wax paper. Allow the glue letters to dry completely, then peel the letters from wax paper.

2. Loop and tie a length of dental floss to each letter to make a hanger.

3. Suspend the letter sun catchers in a window.

Foil Mobile

Materials: aluminum foil, clothes hangers (one for each child), yarn, tape, scissors

Directions:

1. Have each child shape aluminum foil to make four or five letters.

2. Help the children tie a length of yarn to each letter shape. Tape the opposite end of each yarn length to a clothes hanger to create mobiles.

Toothpick Picture Sounds

Materials: colored toothpicks, white paper, glue, crayons or markers

Directions:

1. Have the children glue colored toothpicks into a letter shape at the top of a white sheet of paper.

2. Below the letter, have the students glue additional toothpicks into the shape of an object whose name begins with the sound of that letter. Examples might include the letter **F** with a fish below, the letter **H** with a house below, or the letter **K** with a kite below.

3. Allow the glue to dry, then let the children use markers or crayons to add details to their pictures.

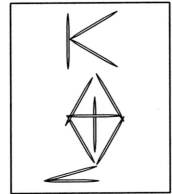

Alphabet Art *(cont.)*

Puzzle Piece Art

Materials: sheets of cardboard, old jigsaw puzzle pieces, glue, yarn

Directions:

1. Cut out a large cardboard letter for each child.

2. Provide the children with glue and old jigsaw puzzle pieces. Have them glue a puzzle piece collage over their cardboard letters.

3. Glue a yarn loop to the back of each letter to make a hanger.

Variation: Divide the class into small groups of children. Proceed in the same manner as above, and have each group construct a puzzle piece letter collage.

Letter Necklace

Materials: poster board, old magazines, glue, colorful sequins or glitter, markers, scissors, paper punch, yarn

Directions:

1. Let each child draw and cut a circle from poster board. Have them each write a letter on one side of their circles and glue a magazine picture cut-out of an item that begins with the sound of that letter on the opposite side.

2. Let them trace their letters with glue, then sprinkle glitter or sequins over the glue.

3. Paper punch a hole at the top of each circle. Thread the hole with yarn and knot the ends of the yarn together to make necklaces.

Alphabet Art *(cont.)*

ABC Hat

Materials: Letter Pocket Cards (page 149), construction paper, scissors, glue, stapler

Directions:

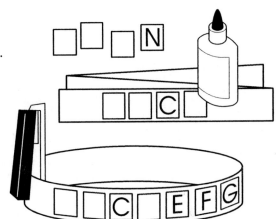

1. Make a copy of the Letter Pocket Cards for each child. Cut construction paper into hat-sized strips, one for each child.

2. Have the children cut the letter blocks apart. Mix up the letters, then glue them onto the hat strips in alphabetical order.

3. Staple the ends of each child's hat strip to size.

Reading Letters

Materials: poster board, alphabet stamps, stamp pads

Directions:

1. Cut a bookmark-sized rectangle of poster board for each child.

2. Have the children use alphabet stamps and colorful stamp pads to stamp letter shapes on both sides of their rectangles. Use these as bookmarks.

Letter Wrap

Materials: large sheets of newsprint paper, sponges cut into alphabet shapes, tempera paint in various colors, water

Directions:

1. Add a little water to thin different colors of tempera paint in several containers.

2. Have the children use the letter-shaped sponges to stamp letters over large sheets of newsprint.

3. Allow the sheets to dry, then use the pages to wrap gifts.

Variation: Use bright colors on black and white sheets of newspaper. Proceed in the same manner as above.

Alphabet Art *(cont.)*

Letter Mosaic

Materials: corrugated cardboard, dried green peas and red kidney beans, marker, glue, yarn

Directions:

1. Cut a corrugated cardboard square for each child. Have the children write a letter on each of their squares, then trace over their letters with glue. Let them set dried green peas into the glue to shape the letter. Allow the glued letters to dry.

2. Let the children spread glue over their cardboard squares around their letters, then cover this glue with dried red kidney beans.

3. When dry, glue a yarn loop to the back of each square to make a hanger.

Initial Necklaces

Materials: letter patterns or stencils, construction paper, markers, scissors, paper punch, yarn or ribbon

Directions:

1. Have the children trace around a pattern or use stencils to draw their initials on construction paper. Cut these letters out. Use a paper punch to make a hole at the top of each letter.

2. Let the children use markers to decorate their letters.

3. Help the students string their letters onto lengths of yarn or ribbon to make necklaces.

Variation: Make Initial Necklaces to use as gifts for parents, grandparents, siblings, etc.

Alphabet Art (cont.)

Flower Pot Letters

Materials: small clay flower pots (one for each child), permanent markers, plastic sandwich bags with twist-ties, potting soil, ribbon, packets of seeds (one for each child)

Directions:

1. Have the children use permanent markers to draw colorful letter shapes over the outside of their clay pots.

2. Help the students place potting soil into plastic sandwich bags, twist-tie the bags shut, then tie a ribbon bow over the twist-tie.

3. Let the children place their bags of soil into their flowerpots with a packet of seeds.

4. Send the pots home as special gifts for Mom.

Paperweight Letters

Materials: prepared craft dough, baking racks, tempera or craft acrylic paint in various colors, paint brushes, clear acrylic sealer (spray or brush-on)

Directions:

1. Provide each child with a small portion of prepared craft dough. Help the children use their craft dough to shape a letter **D** for Dad.

2. Set the craft dough shapes on a baking rack and allow them to dry completely. Turn them over daily so they will dry flat.

3. When dry, these can be painted, then sprayed or brushed with clear acrylic paint to seal.

4. Send the paperweights home as a special gift for Dad.

Food for Thought

Children and Food: Eating nutritious foods enhances the physical and mental growth of children. Food preparation activities allow us to teach positive eating habits during the early years of development so children will be able to make better choices later in life. Our job is not to force children to eat, but to encourage them to try a variety of foods. Cooking activities directly involve the children in the preparation of their snacks so that they will be more likely to taste everything.

Learning Through Cooking: Because food preparation involves all five senses, it is an excellent way for young children to learn. Food explorations are easily incorporated into the academic curriculum, making them multi-purpose learning experiences. Skills children can develop include the following:

1. **Language:** Children can learn new words, increasing the range of their vocabularies. They will also be involved in following oral directions, communicating with each other, learning to read recipes, and following sequential order.

2. **Science:** Students can observe chemical change first-hand, become aware of how they use their five senses to learn about the world around them, and develop a sense of good nutrition.

3. **Math:** Recipes involve children in measuring and counting. Students are also introduced to fractions.

4. **Social Awareness:** Children learn to cooperate and take turns in group situations.

5. **Health and Safety:** Students also learn the correct way to use any necessary equipment and the importance of working with clean hands and tools, on clean surfaces.

Cooking is a relaxed and enjoyable way to learn. These activities help children build their self-confidence by providing them with a sense of accomplishment.

Food for Thought (cont.)

Preparation for Cooking Activities:

1. Choose a majority of activities that are immediately edible, as young children are not fond of waiting.

2. Select simple recipes that make use of few ingredients. This will save time and confusion in the preparation, production, and clean up of activities.

3. Assemble all necessary ingredients and equipment before you begin.

4. The first step in any food preparation activity should always be washing hands.

5. When you begin, read the recipe to the students, displaying ingredients and equipment as you name them. As you work through the recipe, explain and demonstrate any cooking terms, such as "dice," "beat," "chop," "slice," etc.

6. Help children feel successful by teaching them how to safely use the utensils as they do most of the work.

7. Involve the children in the whole process of cooking, from set-up to clean-up.

8. Provide a calm, relaxed, pleasant atmosphere for a positive eating experience and encourage the use of good table manners.

Allergy Awareness: Some children in your class may be allergic to certain foods, such as peanut oil, milk products, strawberries, etc. It is very important to be aware of these allergies when planning any cooking activity. Keep a list of these children and their allergies posted for easy reference. In the following recipes, alternative ingredients have been suggested where feasible. Another consideration may be to ask the allergic child's parents to provide a very special snack for their child on cooking day, or to provide substitute ingredients, such as lactose-free milk, for their child to use. A final consideration would be to simply choose a different recipe. In addition to being prepared for possible allergies, use this opportunity to teach your children about what happens when we are allergic to certain substances.

Alphabet Snacks

Letter Stir-Ups

Ingredients: instant oatmeal, water, fruit chunks or pieces, milk (optional)

Directions:

1. Prepare instant oatmeal as directed on package, making one bowl for each child.

2. Prepare and set out chosen fruit for the children to use. Choose fruit appropriate for the letter you wish to emphasize, such as raisins for **R**, peach chunks for **P**, apple chunks for **A**, etc.

3. When the oatmeal has cooled sufficiently, have the children set the fruit pieces onto the surface of the oatmeal in the shape of the appropriate letter.

4. After everyone has shaped a letter, let the children stir the fruit pieces into their oatmeal before eating.

5. Add milk, if desired.

Toast Letter Shapes

Ingredients: wheat or white bread slices, softened cream cheese, raisins, food color

Directions:

1. Toast a slice of bread for each child. Have the children press cookie cutters into their toast slices to cut a shape such as a sun or an apple.

2. Tint the softened cream cheese with a food color to correspond with the toast shape, such as yellow for the sun or red for the apple. Help the children spread the tinted cream cheese over their toast shapes.

3. Have the children use raisins to make a letter on their toast shapes. For example, they would make an **S** on the sun and an **A** on the apple.

Variation: Substitute other spreadables for certain shapes. For example, they might spread strawberry jam on an apple shape and peanut butter on a dog shape. Try buttering a bear shape, then sprinkling it with a cinnamon-sugar mixture.

Alphabet Snacks *(cont.)*

Rainbow Letters

Ingredients: white bread slices, milk, food color, butter or margarine

Directions:

1. Pour a small amount of milk into several different bowls. Use food color to tint each container of milk a different color.

2. Have the children use cotton swabs to paint a colored milk letter on a slice of white bread, then toast the bread slices.

3. Help the children spread butter or margarine over their warm rainbow slices before eating.

Iced Letters

Ingredients: small tubes of icing in various colors and party cookies, cupcakes, or brownies

Directions:

1. Show the children how to squeeze gently on an icing tube to make the icing flow, as you demonstrate how to shape a letter.

2. Let the children use the tubes of icing to make their own letter decorations on prepared party food.

Pretzel Shapes

Ingredients: pretzel sticks, twists, and circles

Directions:

1. Challenge the children to break pretzels as necessary, then fit their shapes together to make a letter.

2. Have them name each pretzel letter they construct before they eat it.

Name Crackers

Ingredients: graham crackers, peanut butter or other spreadable (jam or cream cheese), alphabet shaped cereal

Directions:

1. Help the children spread peanut butter over their graham crackers.

2. Let them press alphabet shaped cereal into the peanut butter to spell their names.

Alphabet Snacks *(cont.)*

Baked Letters

Ingredients: biscuit baking mix, milk or water, two egg whites, sesame or poppy seeds, butter or margarine, jam

Directions:

1. Prepare baking mix with milk or water, according to package directions. Divide the dough to provide each child with a small portion.

2. Have the children knead the dough and shape it into letters. Place the letters on a baking sheet.

3. Let the children use their clean fingers to spread egg white over their dough letters.

4. Sprinkle sesame or poppy seeds onto the egg white, then bake the letter biscuits according to package directions. Cool before spreading with butter, margarine or jam.

Fruit Rounds

Ingredients: English muffins, peanut butter or other spreadable, berries or fruit

Directions:

1. Slice and toast the English muffins to make one round for each child. Help the children spread their round with peanut butter, cream cheese, or jam.

2. Let the children press berries or fruit pieces into the muffin topping to shape a letter. For example, use blueberries to shape a **B** or pineapple pieces to make a **P**.

Build-a-Letter

Ingredients: pretzel sticks, cheese cubes or grapes

Directions:

1. Let the children connect the pretzels into letter shapes by sticking the ends of the pretzel sticks into cheese cubes or grapes.

2. Have the children name their constructed letters before they eat them.

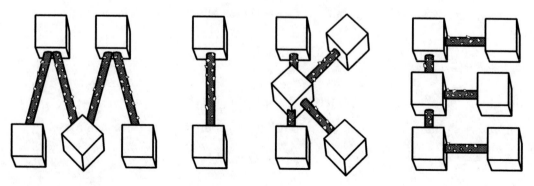

Alphabet Snacks *(cont.)*

Pizza Letters

Ingredients: hamburger rolls, tomato sauce, cheese slices

Directions:

1. Divide each hamburger roll into two rounds. Toast the hamburger rounds under a broiler or in a toaster oven. Provide each child with one round.
2. Help the children spread tomato sauce over their rounds.
3. Let the children use the letter shaped cookie cutters to make letters from cheese slices.
4. Top each round with one cheese letter. Heat these letter pizzas under a broiler or in a toaster oven until the cheese begins to melt. Cool before serving.

Letters and Tomato

Ingredients: lettuce, tomato slices, mayonnaise in a squeeze bottle, bread slices

Directions:

1. Distribute one slice of bread to each child. Have each child rip a lettuce leaf to place on his/her bread slice. Have them each set a tomato slice onto the lettuce.
2. Let them each use the squeeze bottle of mayonnaise to draw a letter shape on his/her tomato slice. Have them read their letters.
3. Top the sandwich with a second slice of bread. Cut each into 2–4 sections before eating.

Griddle Letters

Ingredients: complete pancake mix, water or milk, butter or margarine, syrup and/or jam

Directions:

1. Prepare pancake mix as directed on package using milk or water. Pour pancake batter into a squeeze bottle.
2. Squeeze the batter onto a hot griddle to make letter shaped pancakes.
3. Serve the letter cakes with butter, margarine, syrup, and/or jam.

Alphabet Snacks *(cont.)*

Search and Nibble

Ingredients: cans of alphabet soup or boxes of alphabet cereal, water or milk (as necessary)

Directions:

1. Prepare soup as directed on the can, or have the children help to prepare individual bowls of cereal. Cool the soup before eating.

2. Invite the children to name the letters they find as they are eating. Write down the letters they find. Can the class eat the whole alphabet?

Roll-Ups

Ingredients: white or wheat bread slices, peanut butter or cream cheese, jam-filled squeeze bottles

Directions:

1. Have the children use their hands to flatten a slice of bread. Help them spread peanut butter or cream cheese over their flattened slices.

2. Let them use jam-filled squeeze bottles to write a letter shape on these slices.

3. Have them name their letters, then help them to roll up their slices before eating.

Vegetable Salad

Ingredients: lettuce, cottage cheese, vegetable pieces

Directions:

1. Have each child place a lettuce leaf on a plate. Top it with cottage cheese, flattening the surface of the cottage cheese slightly.

2. Let the children use vegetable pieces to make a letter shape on their cottage cheese. For example, use carrot slices to make **C** or pepper chunks to make **P**.

Celebrating Sounds, Shapes and Cultures

Sounds: Serve foods that emphasize certain sounds.

Some examples are listed here:

Aa—apples, applesauce, apricots, avocados

Bb—berries, breads, bananas, beans

Cc—cucumbers, corn, cornbread, carrots

Dd—date nut bread, dates, doughnuts

Ee—egg salad, English muffins, eggnog

Ff—fondue, fig bars, fish sticks

Gf—graham crackers, garlic bread, grapes, gumbo

Hh—hot dog buns, ham, hot dogs, honey

Ii—ice cream, Irish stew, iced cookies

Jj—jam, juice, jelly roll cake, jelly beans

Kk—kiwi, fruit kabobs, kidney beans, ketchup

Ll—lemonade, lentil soup, lettuce

Mm—mandarin oranges, mashed potatoes, melon

Nn—nectarines, noodles, nuts, nut bread

Oo—oatmeal, olives, oranges, oyster crackers

Pp—pancakes, pickles, popcorn, peas, peaches

Qq—quiche, quince jelly, quick bread

Rr—raisins, rice, rye bread, rolls, relish

Ss—sunflower seeds, squash, strawberries

Tt—tuna, toast, tangerines, tomatoes, tapioca

Uu—upside-down cake

Vv—vanilla yogurt, vegetable soup

Ww—waffles, walnuts, watermelon, wild rice

Xx—box drinks, individually boxed snacks

Yy—yogurt, yellow squash, yams

Zz—zucchini, zucchini bread, zwieback toast

Shapes: Serve foods that are shaped like certain letters, such as pineapple slices, doughnuts or bagels for **O**, croissants, crescent rolls, or mandarin orange slices for **C**. For a special treat, serve mini candy canes for **J**.

Multi-Cultural: Invite the parents of students from different cultures to come to school and share a recipe from their homeland with the class. Parents may be able to share recipes for such foods as latkes, egg rolls, quesadillas, or tacos for the children to help prepare and taste.

A Word About Centers . . .

A center is an area of the classroom that contains materials which allow the children to focus their efforts on specific activities, such as math or art. Centers encourage active learning. Materials within each center can change from time to time to correlate with units covered by the class. For example, when you work on a unit about bears, books about this topic will be prominent in your Library Center. Other center materials may remain throughout the school year as they provide ongoing learning experiences, such as those materials that invite children to explore letters, sounds, and words as part of your reading readiness program.

Center Preparation

1. Choose center materials that correlate with the children's developmental abilities.

2. Use only safe, non-toxic materials. Check centers periodically for broken items or small pieces that may be potentially hazardous.

3. Make use of self-correcting materials, whenever possible.

4. Be sure that the children know how to use the various materials at each center.

5. Provide storage at child's eye level to facilitate both play and clean up.

Center Learning

1. Centers allow children to interact and cooperate with others, as well as to work independently at their own pace.

2. Centers encourage communication and active use of the imagination.

3. Use of centers helps children learn to be more independent, make their own decisions, and solve their own problems.

On the following pages you will find suggestions for incorporating reading readiness materials at each center. These should be considered long-term materials, as learning to read is an ongoing process.

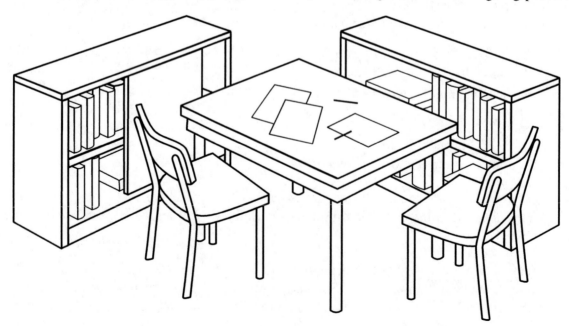

Alphabet Centers

To help children understand the importance of letters and words, and demonstrate how letters and words are integrated into everyday experiences, find ways to incorporate the printed word in each of your centers. Center suggestions for increasing the children's exposure to written language are listed below.

Building Center

1. Label the various shapes of blocks.
2. Photograph individual children's projects. Mount, label, and display the pictures in the center.
3. Provide roadside signs for use with vehicles.
4. Help the children print labels for their creations.

Art Center

1. In addition to your regular art supplies, include letter stamps and stencils, pencils, and lined paper.
2. Collect and offer greeting, thank you, and plain note cards. invitations, postcards, and envelopes.
3. Provide picture word cards for children who wish to practice writing words.

Science Center

1. Provide journals for recording experiment progress.
2. Supply science alphabet books, a weather chart, life cycle charts, nature magazines, and crayons for rubbings.

Math Center

1. Include calendars, appointment books, sales slip books, a phone book, numeral word cards, grocery flyers, and mail order catalogs.

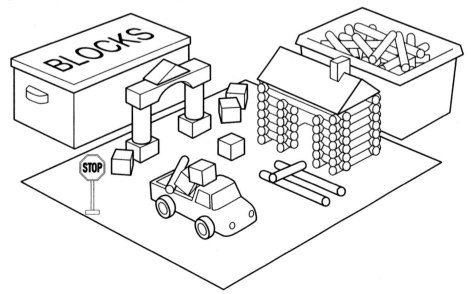

Alphabet Centers *(cont.)*

Library

1. Display a variety of books and magazines for the children to look at. Slip a sign-out card into each book and provide a date stamp to use so the children can borrow books and know when to return them.

2. Set up a flannel board supplied with colorful felt letters.

3. Provide chart paper and markers for children to practice writing letters and words.

Family Center

Letters and words can be found in numerous places around the house. Offer children a phone book, an address book, food cans, cartons, and boxes with labels, magazines, newspapers, a television program guide, a cookbook, pencils, a grocery/note pad, and a small bulletin board for posting messages. For extra fun, add a "while you were out" message pad by the toy telephone.

Center Signs

Copy the signs on the following pages for use in labeling your centers. Color the signs if you wish, and mount each on cardboard. Suspend the signs from the ceiling or mount them on a wall in each center. Call the children's attention to the words, letters, and pictures on each sign. Talk about how the illustrations are clues to what the words say.

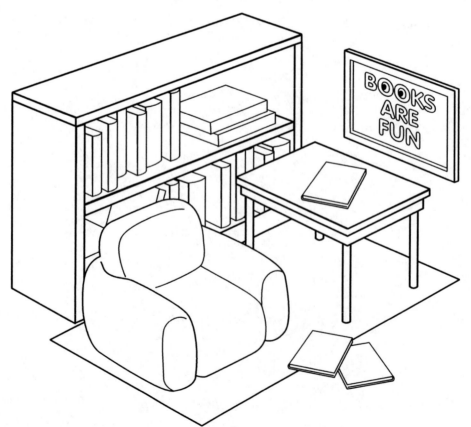

Building

Art

Science

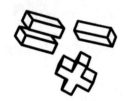 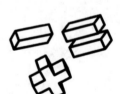

Math

 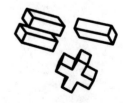

Library

Family

Name: _____

alligator

Color

a – green

b – brown

Cut and glue on another
piece of paper to make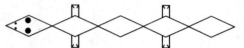

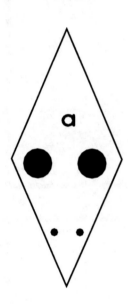
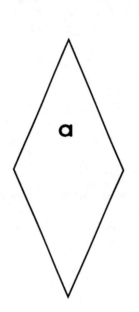
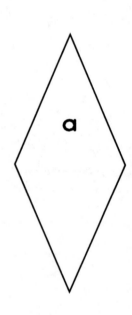

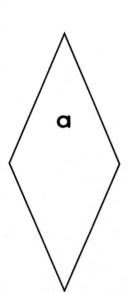
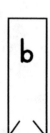
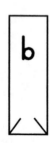
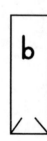
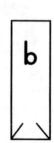
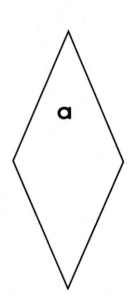

Letter Search Bubbles

Aa

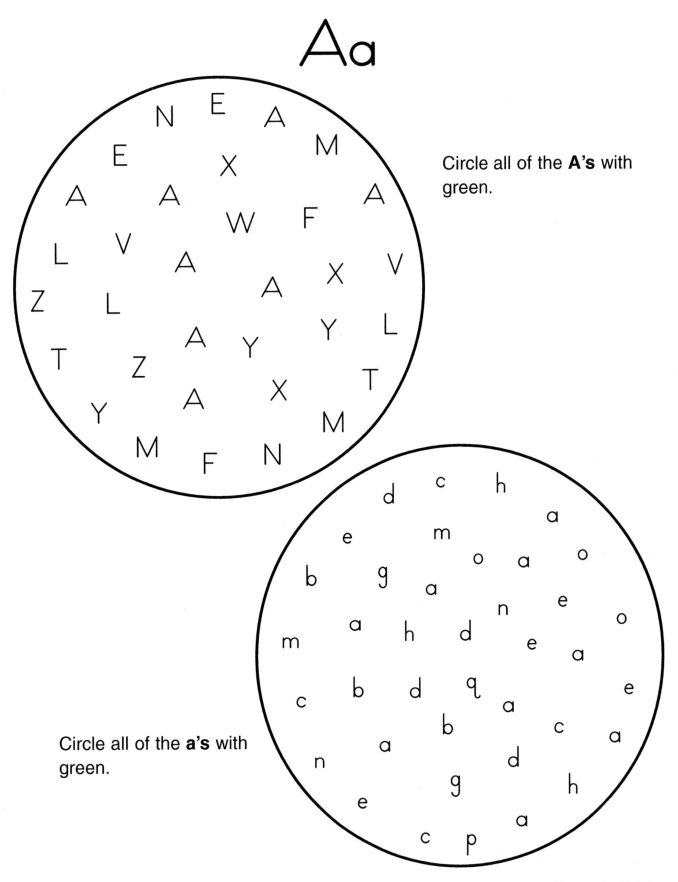

Circle all of the **A's** with green.

Circle all of the **a's** with green.

Name: _____

Color red.

A

Trace

1↙ A ↘2
3→

A A A

Trace

a

1↖ ↓2 a

a a a

Write

A

Write

a

Draw a picture of something that begins with the sound of **A**.

Color it red.

Name: _____

bee

Color

a – yellow

b – black

Cut and glue on another piece of paper to make

Don't forget to add antennae.

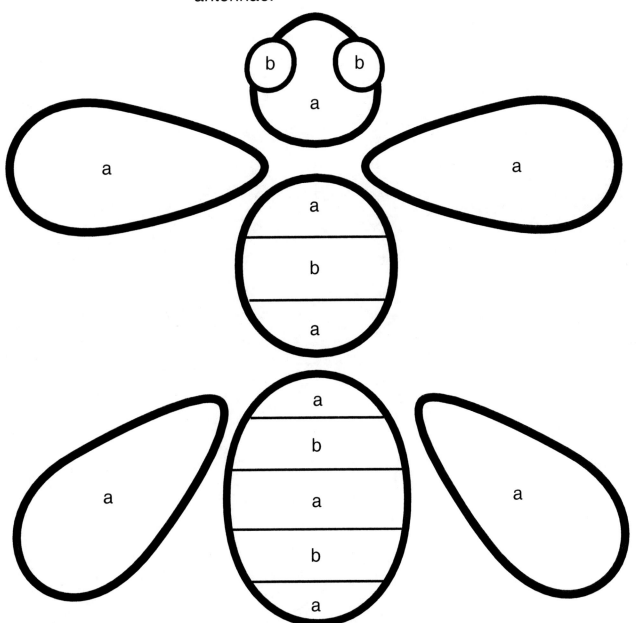

Name: _____

Letter Search Bubbles

Bb

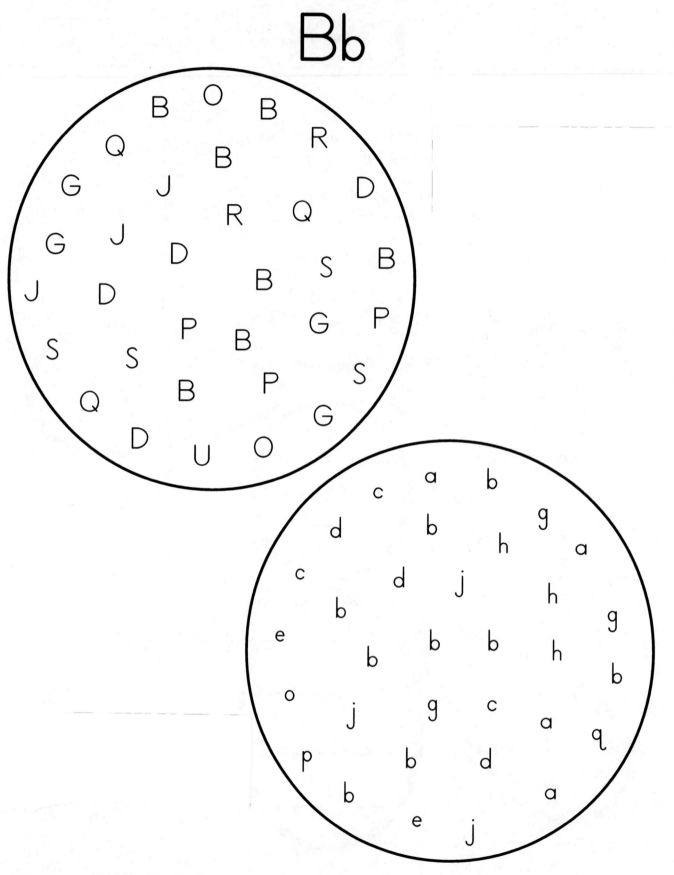

Name: _____

Color blue.

Trace

Trace

Write

Write

Draw a picture of something that begins with the sound of **B**.

Color it blue.

Name: _____

_____

car

Color

a – red

b – yellow

c – brown

Cut and glue on another piece of paper to make

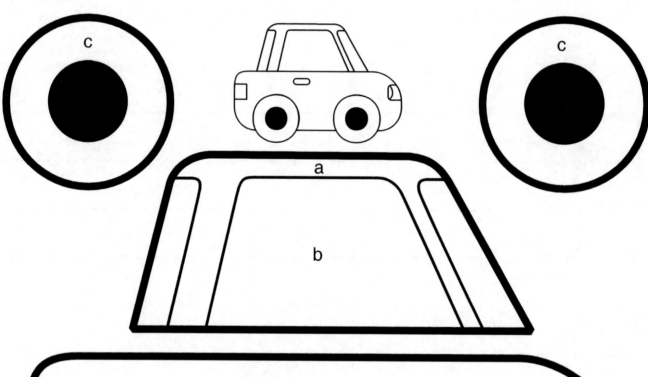

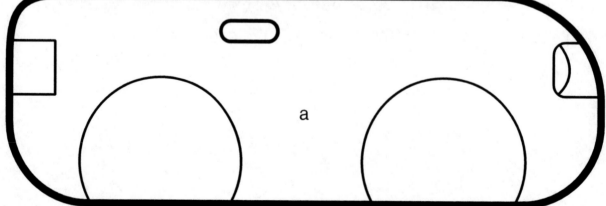

Letter Search Bubbles

Cc

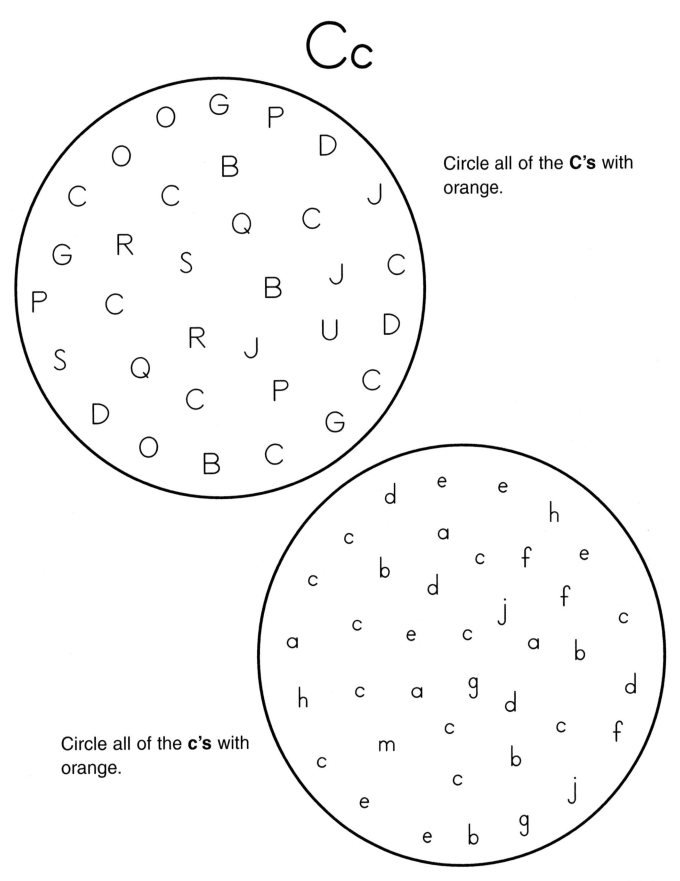

Circle all of the **C's** with orange.

Circle all of the **c's** with orange.

Name: ______________________________

Color yellow.

C

Trace

C C C

Trace

c

c c c c

Write

C

Write

c

Draw a picture of something that begins with the sound of **C**.

Color it yellow.

dog

Color

b – brown

c – yellow

d – black

Cut and glue on another piece of paper to make

Don't forget to add whiskers to your dog.

Letter Search Bubbles

Dd

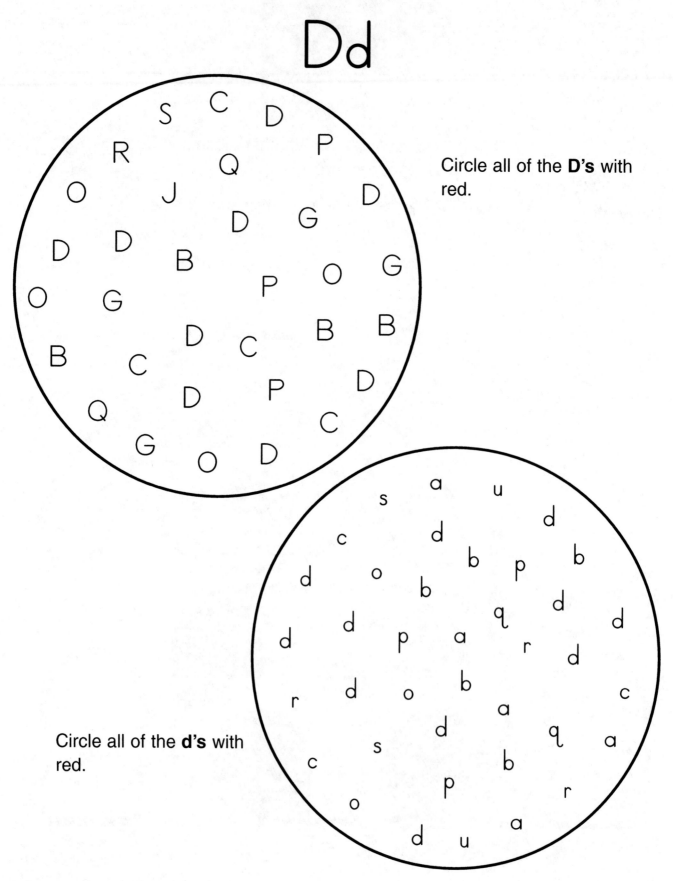

Circle all of the **D's** with red.

Circle all of the **d's** with red.

54

Name:

Color green.

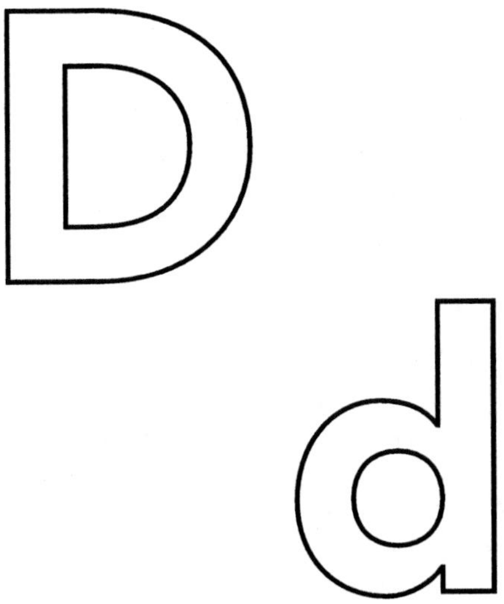

Trace

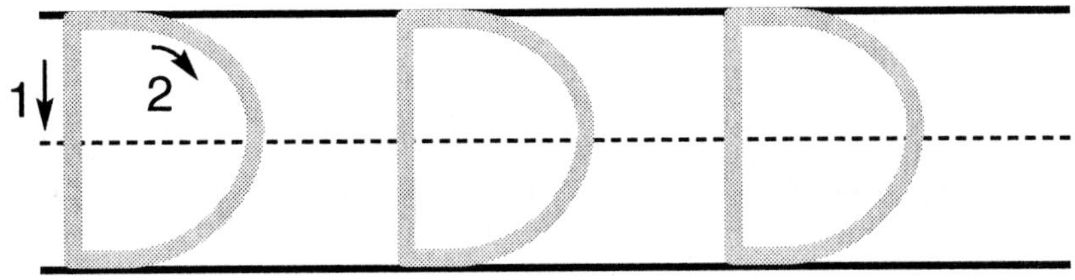

D

1↓ 2↗ D D D D

Trace

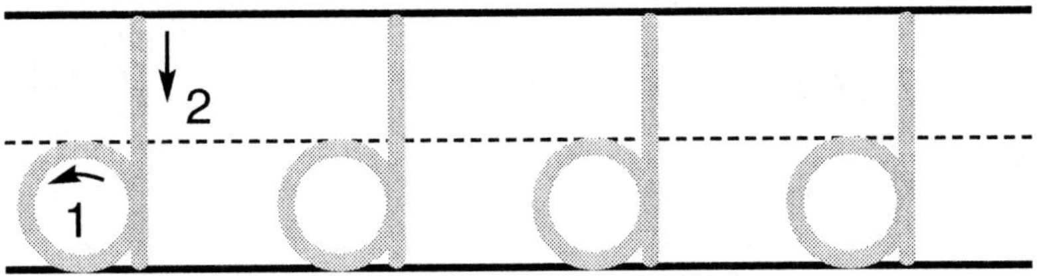

d

↓2 d d d d
1↖

Write

D

Write

d

Draw a picture of something that begins with the sound of **D**.

Color it green.

eggs

Color.

d – yellow

e – blue

Cut and glue on another piece of paper to make

Letter Search Bubbles

Ee

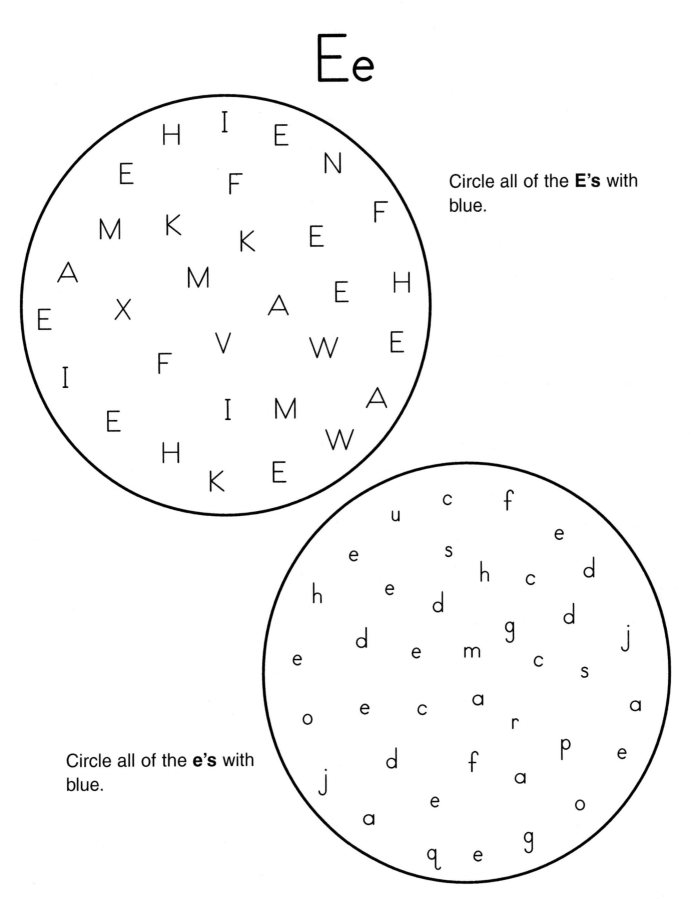

Circle all of the **E's** with blue.

Circle all of the **e's** with blue.

Name: ____________________

Color orange.

E

e

Trace

E E E

Trace

e e e e

Write

E

Write

e

Draw a picture of something that begins with the sound of **E**.

Color it orange.

fish

Color

c – yellow

d – green

e – orange

f – brown

Cut and glue on another piece of paper to make

Don't forget to draw a bowl for your fish.

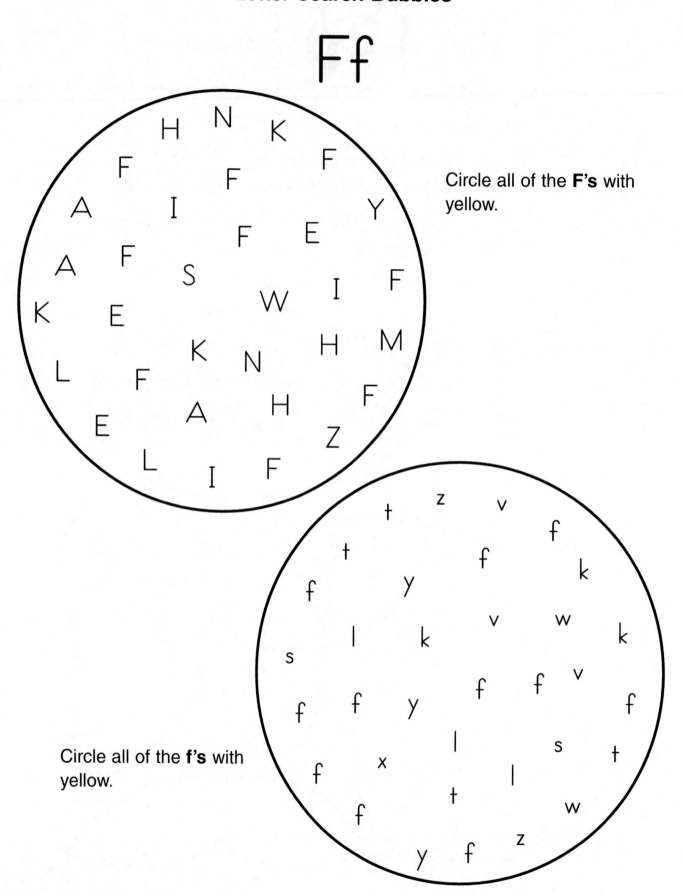

Name: _____

Letter Search Bubbles

Ff

Circle all of the **F's** with yellow.

Circle all of the **f's** with yellow.

Name: _____

Color purple.

Trace

Trace

Write

Write

Draw a picture of something that begins with the sound of **F**.

Color it purple.

Name: _____

gifts

Color

b – blue

c – yellow

d – red

e – purple

f – green

g – orange

Cut and glue on another piece of paper to make

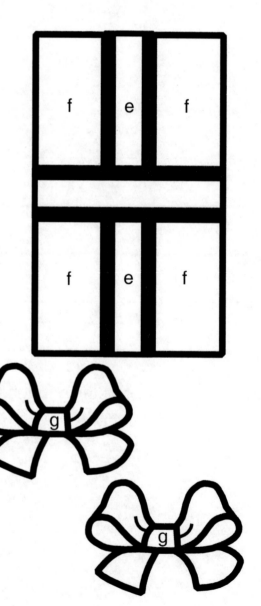

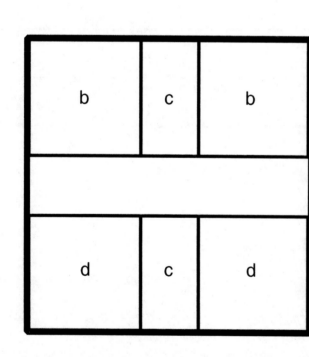

Name: _____

Letter Search Bubbles

Gg

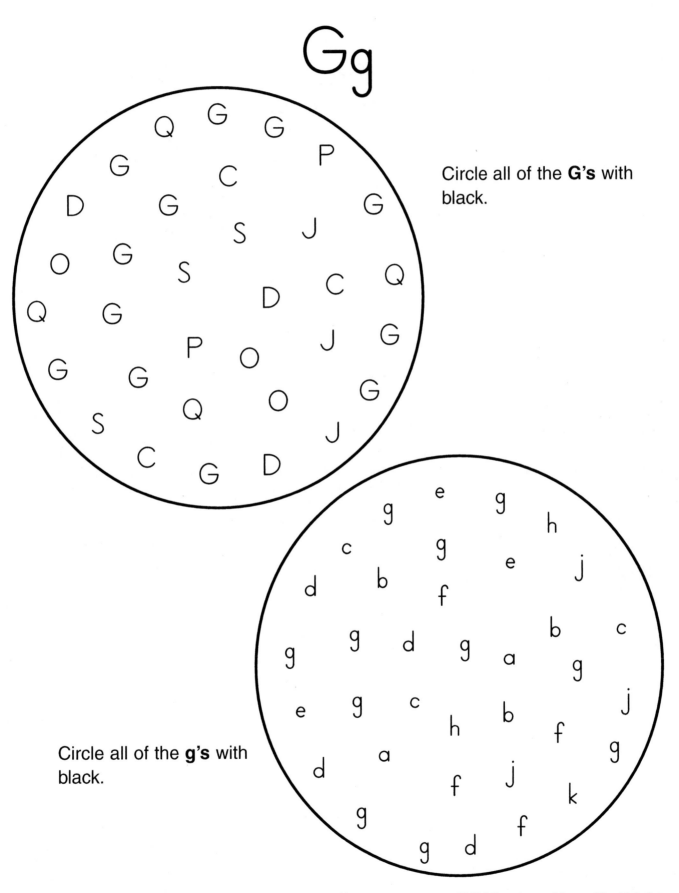

Circle all of the **G's** with black.

Circle all of the **g's** with black.

Name: _____

Color brown.

Trace

G   G   G   G

Trace

g   g   g   g   g

Write

G

Write

g

Draw a picture of something that begins with the sound of **G**.

Color it brown.

Name: _____

house

Color

c – blue

d – brown

e – green

f – red

g – yellow

h – black

Cut and glue on another piece of paper to make

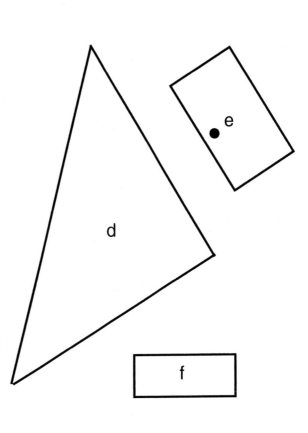

h

c

d

e

f

g

g

Letter Search Bubbles

Hh

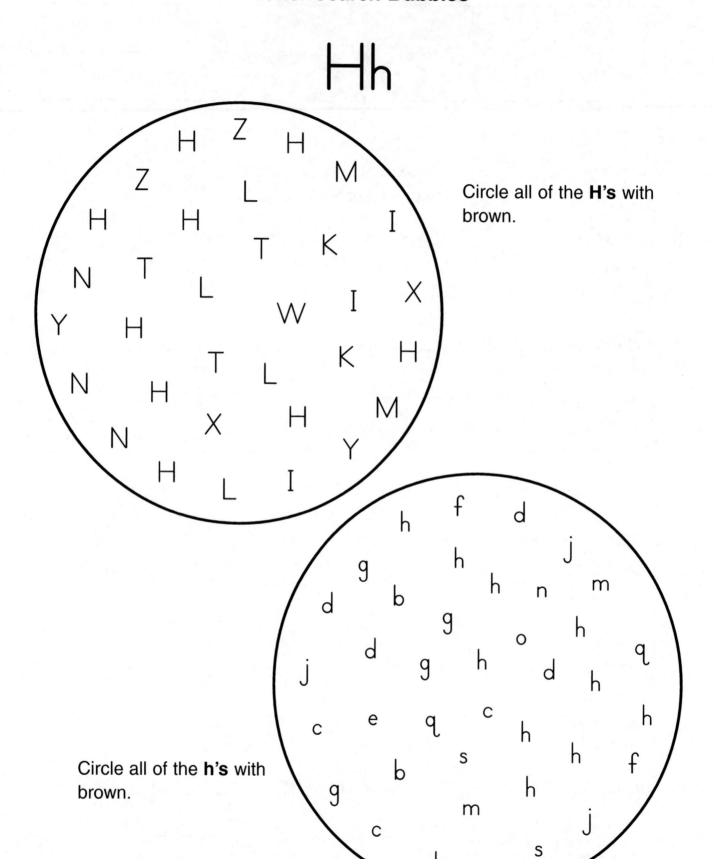

Circle all of the **H's** with brown.

Circle all of the **h's** with brown.

Name: _____

Color black.

Trace

Trace

Write

Write

Draw a picture of something that begins with the sound of **H**.

Color it black.

ice cream

Color
f – brown
g – yellow
h – red
i – orange

Cut and glue on another piece of paper to make

Name: _____

Letter Search Bubbles

Ii

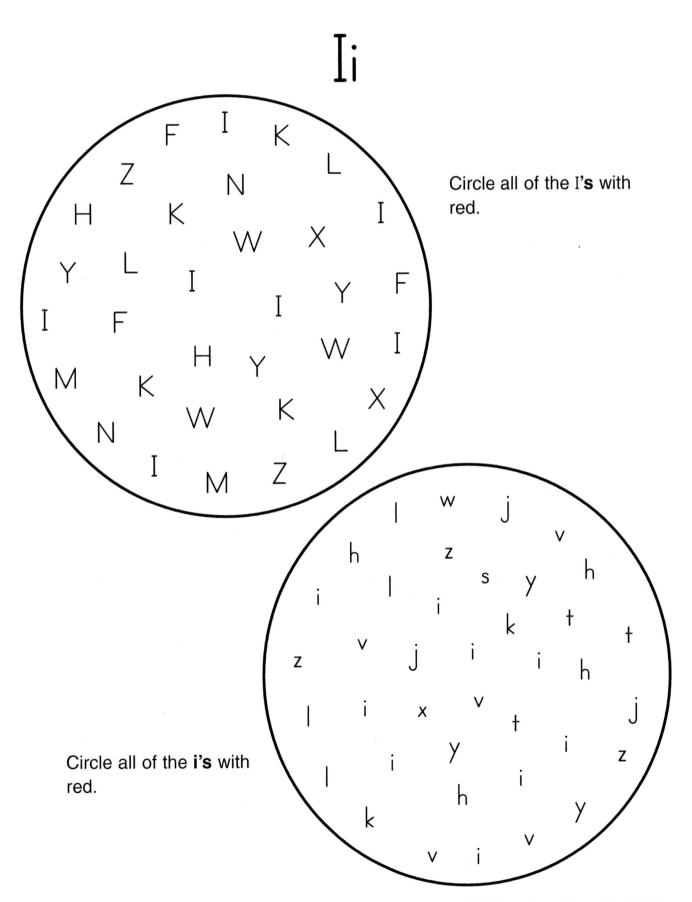

Circle all of the I's with red.

Circle all of the i's with red.

Name: _____

Color red.

Trace

1↓ 2→
3→

Trace

•2

1↓

Write

Write

Draw a picture of something that begins with the sound of **I**.

Color it red.

Name: _____

jet

Color

h – blue

i – red

j – yellow

Cut and glue on another piece of paper to make

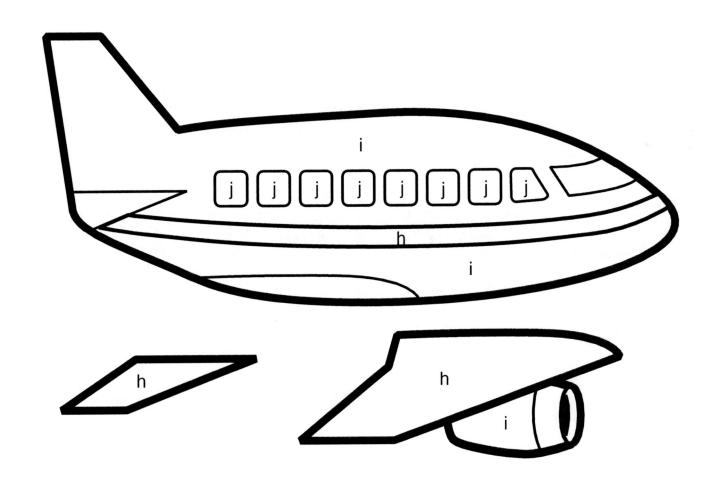

Name: _____

Letter Search Bubbles

Jj

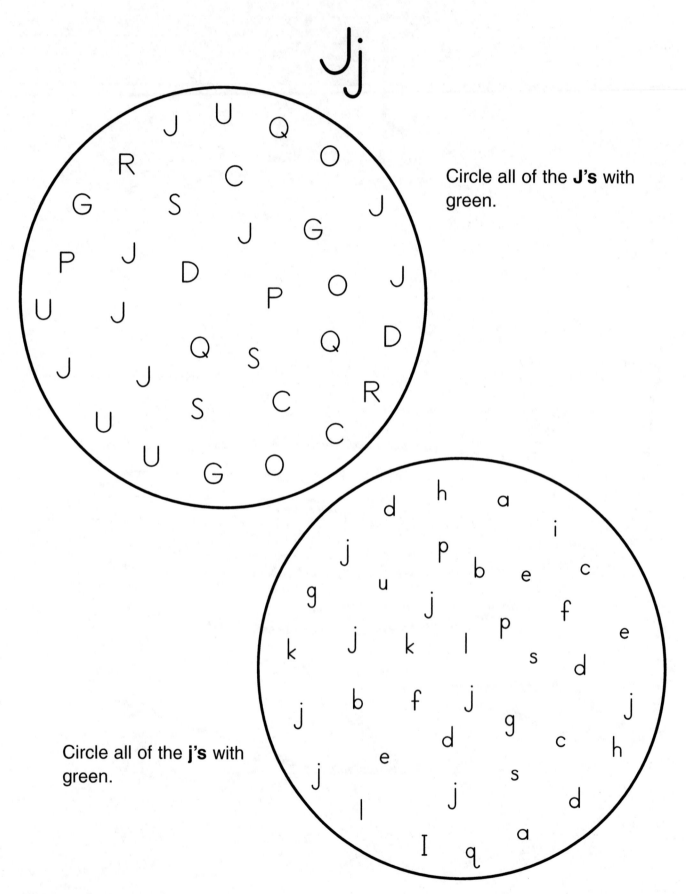

Circle all of the **J's** with green.

Circle all of the **j's** with green.

Color blue.

Trace

J

1↓ J J J J J J

Trace

j

2 • • • • • • •
1↓ j j j j j j j

Write

J

Write

j

Draw a picture of something that begins with the sound of **J**.

Color it blue.

kite

Color

f – orange

g – green

h - red

i – purple

j – yellow

k – blue

Cut and glue on another piece of paper to make

Don't forget to add a piece of yarn for the tail.

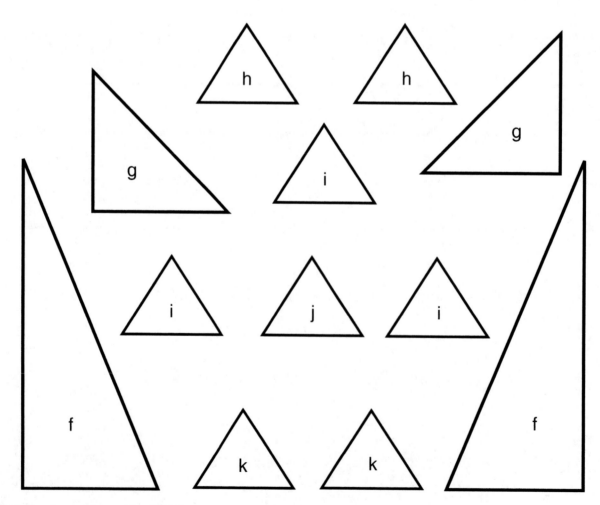

Name: _____

Letter Search Bubbles

Kk

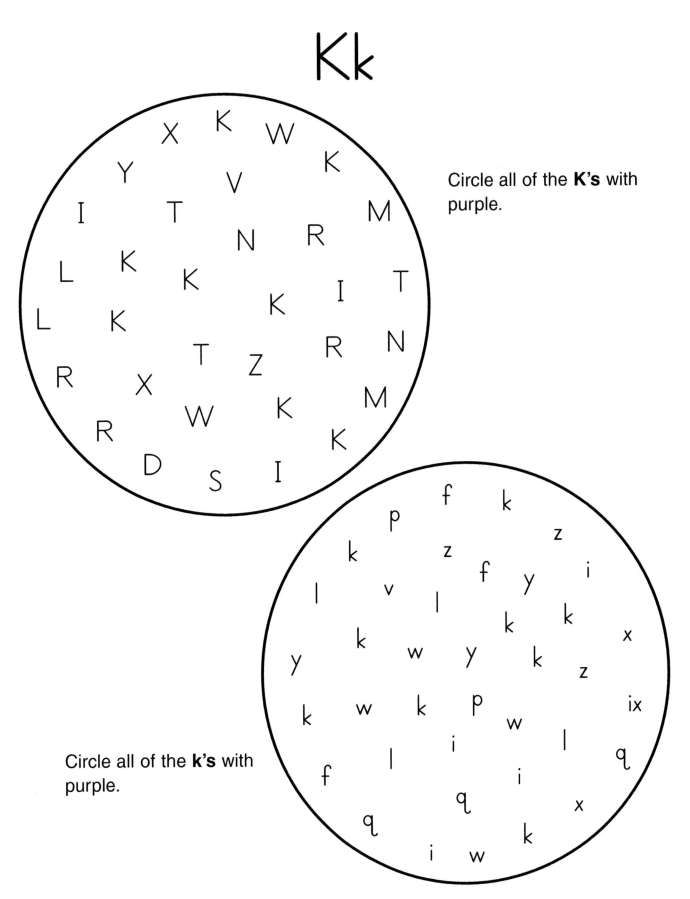

Circle all of the **K's** with purple.

Circle all of the **k's** with purple.

Name: ______________________________

Color yellow.

K

k

Trace

K K K

Trace

k k k k k

Write

K

Write

k

Draw a picture of something that begins with the sound of **K**.

Color it yellow.

Name: _____

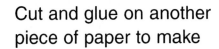 lamp

Color

i – green

j – blue

k – red

l – yellow

Cut and glue on another piece of paper to make

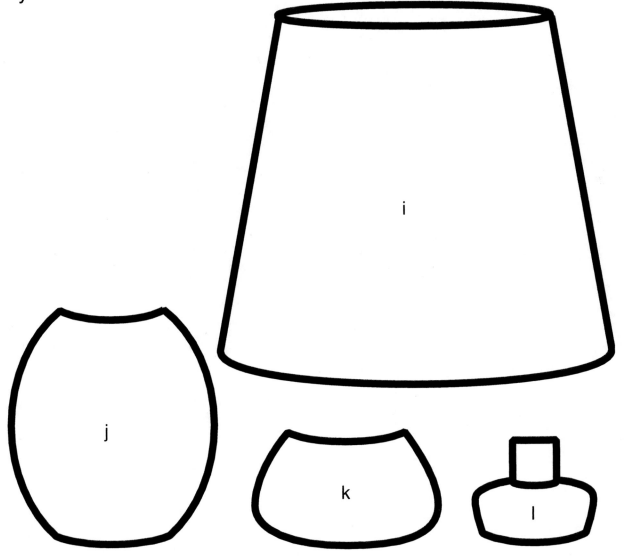

Letter Search Bubbles

Ll

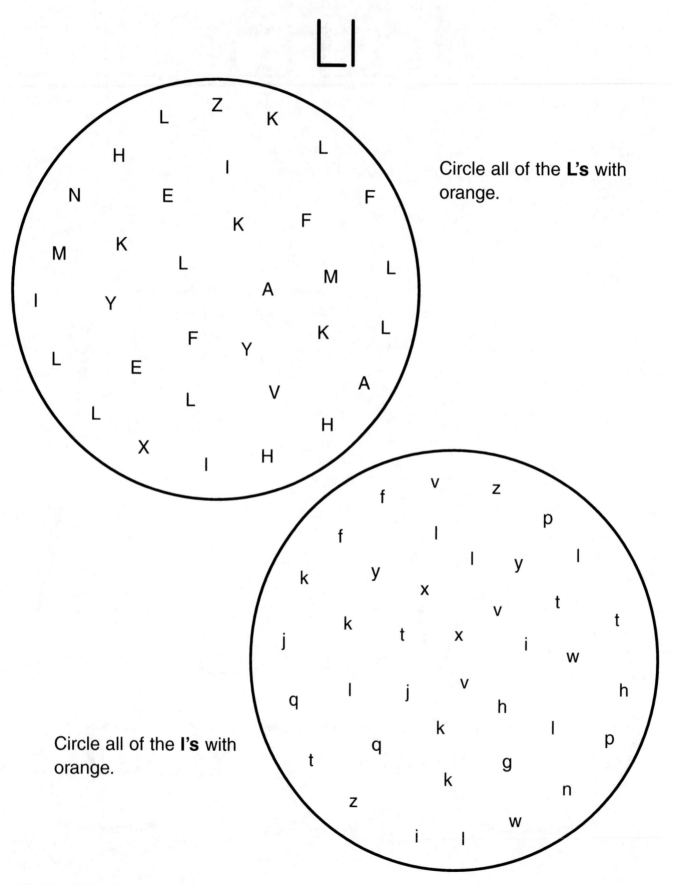

Circle all of the **L's** with orange.

Circle all of the **l's** with orange.

Name: ______________________________

Color green.

Trace

1↓ 2→

Trace

1↓

Write

Write

Draw a picture of something that begins with the sound of **L**.

Color it green.

Name: _____

_____

mouse

Color

k – pink

l – brown

m – black

Cut and glue on another
piece of paper to make

Don't forget to add whiskers.

Letter Search Bubbles

Mm

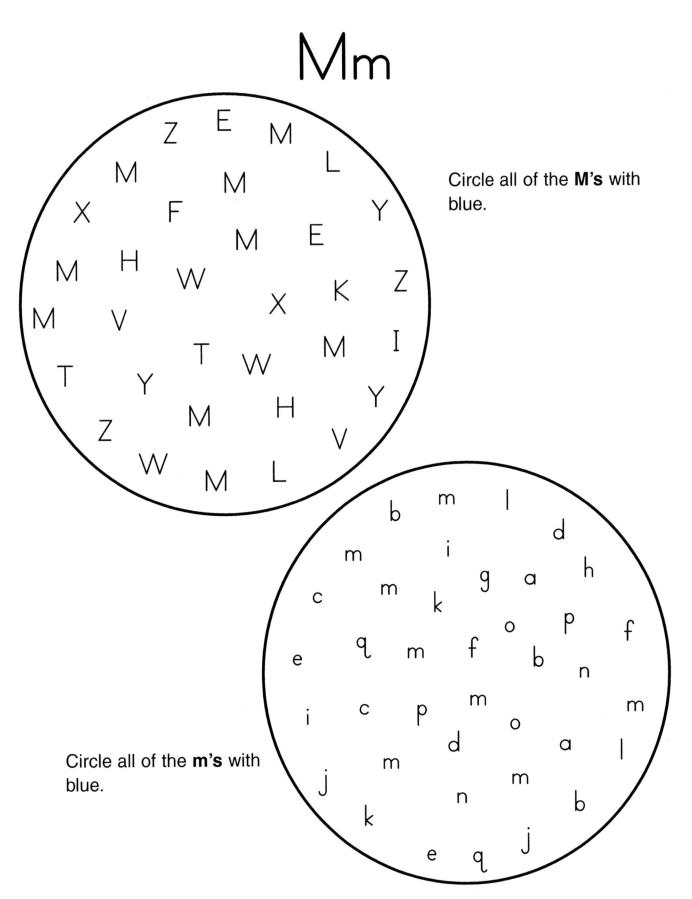

Circle all of the **M's** with blue.

Circle all of the **m's** with blue.

Name: ____________________

Color orange.

M

m

Trace

M M M

Trace

m m m

Write

M

Write

m

Draw a picture of something that begins with the sound of **M**.

Color it orange.

necktie

Color

i – black

j - green

k – yellow

l – blue

m – purple

n – orange

Cut and glue to another piece of paper to make

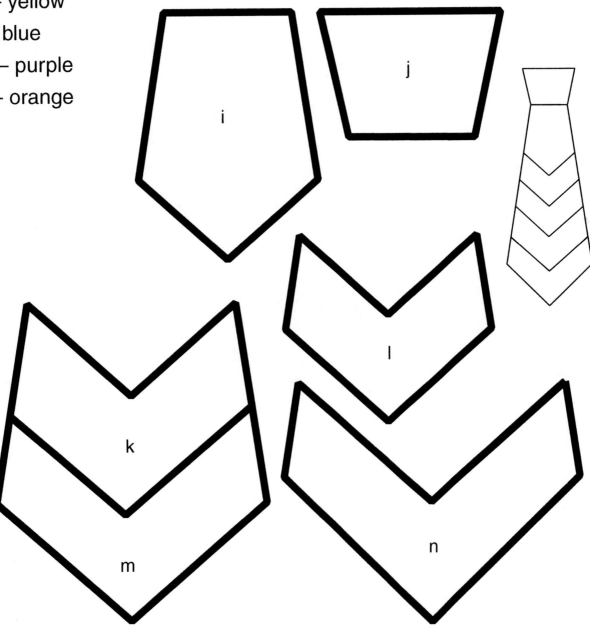

Letter Search Bubbles

Nn

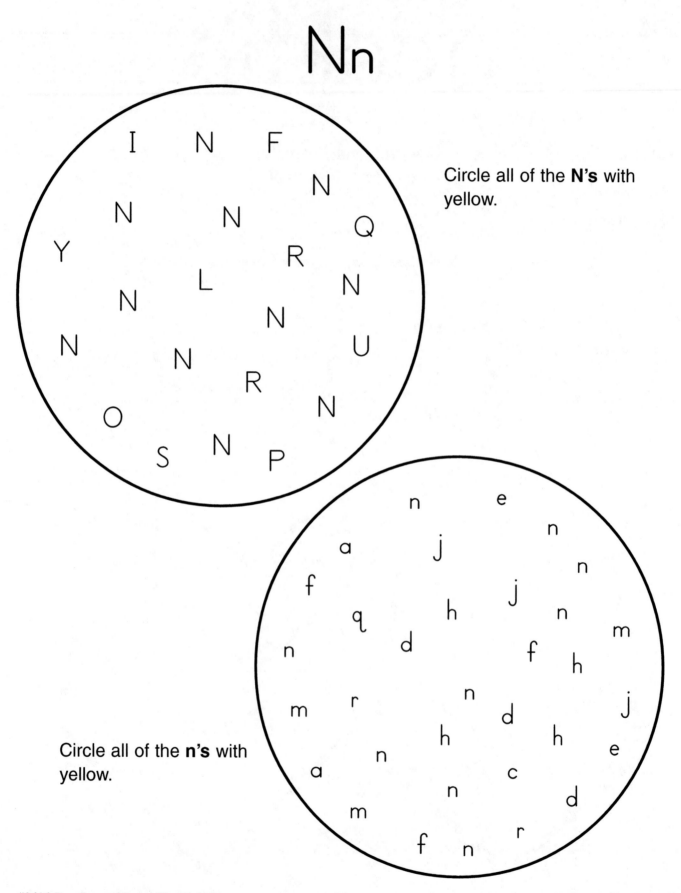

Circle all of the **N's** with yellow.

Circle all of the **n's** with yellow.

84

Name: ____________________

Color purple.

N

n

Trace

1 2 3

N N N

Trace

1 2

n n n n

Write

N

Write

n

Draw a picture of something that begins with the sound of **N**.

Color it purple.

ow

Color

m – brown

n – yellow

o – orange

Cut and glue on another piece of paper to make

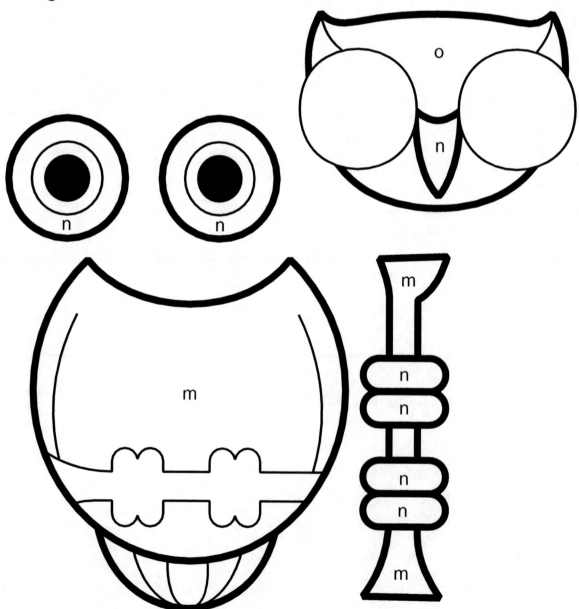

Name: _____

Letter Search Bubbles

Oo

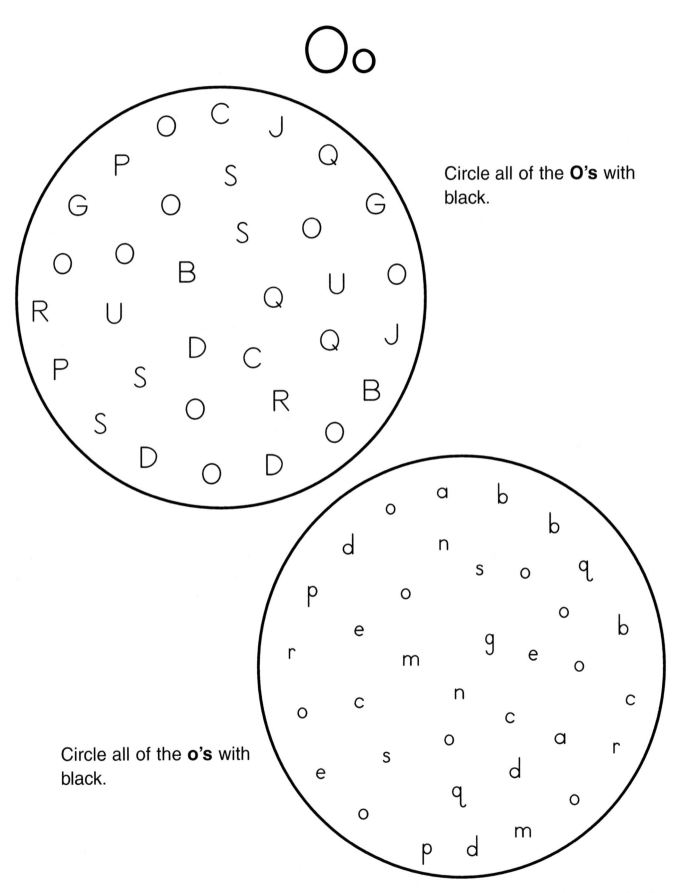

Circle all of the **O's** with black.

Circle all of the **o's** with black.

Name: _____

Color brown.

Trace

Trace

Write

Write

Draw a picture of something that begins with the sound of **O**.

Color it brown.

Name: _____

_____

pig

Color

o – orange

p – pink

Cut and glue on another
piece of paper to make

Don't forget to add a
tail.

Letter Search Bubbles

Pp

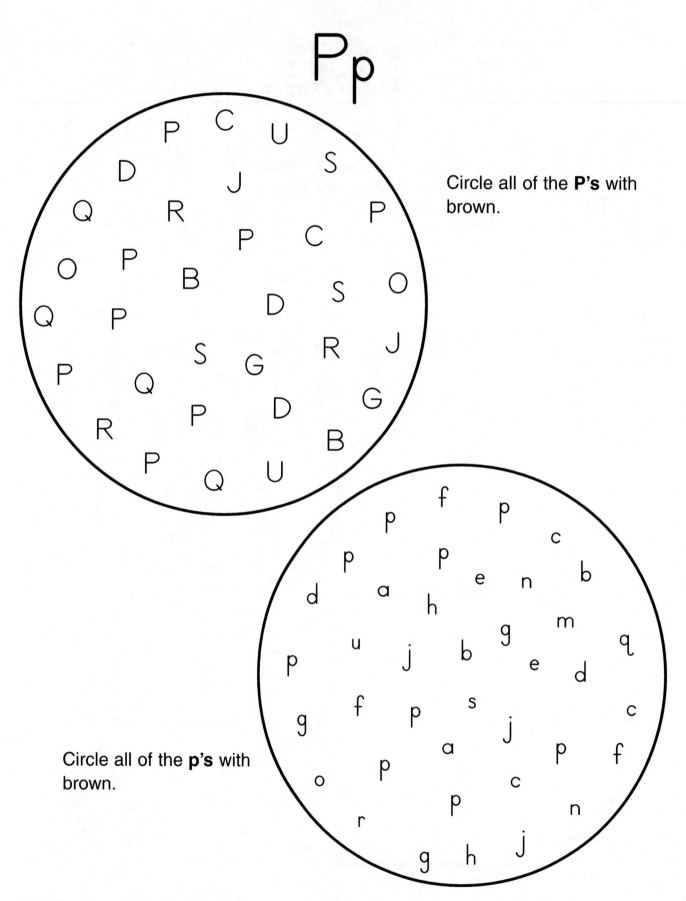

Circle all of the **P's** with brown.

Circle all of the **p's** with brown.

Name: ______________________________

Color black.

P

Trace

1 2 P P P

Trace

1 2 p p p p

p

Write

P

Write

p

Draw a picture of something that begins with the sound of **P**.

Color it black.

Name: _____

quilt

Color

m – red

n – blue

o – yellow

p – green

q – orange

Cut and glue on another piece of paper to make

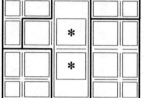

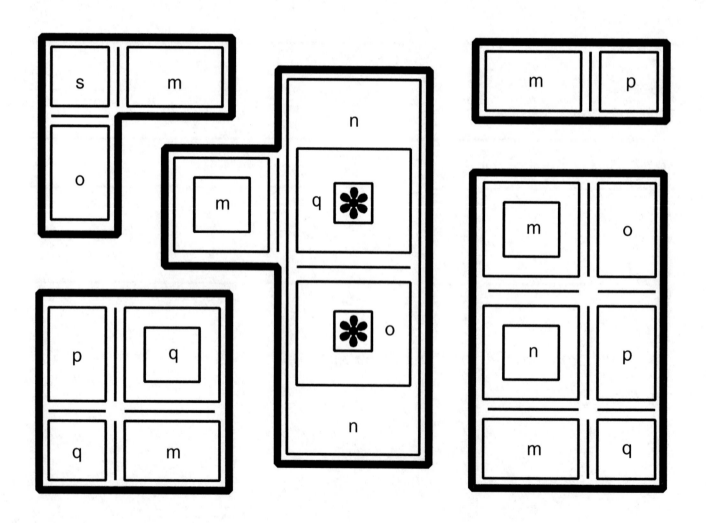

Letter Search Bubbles

Qq

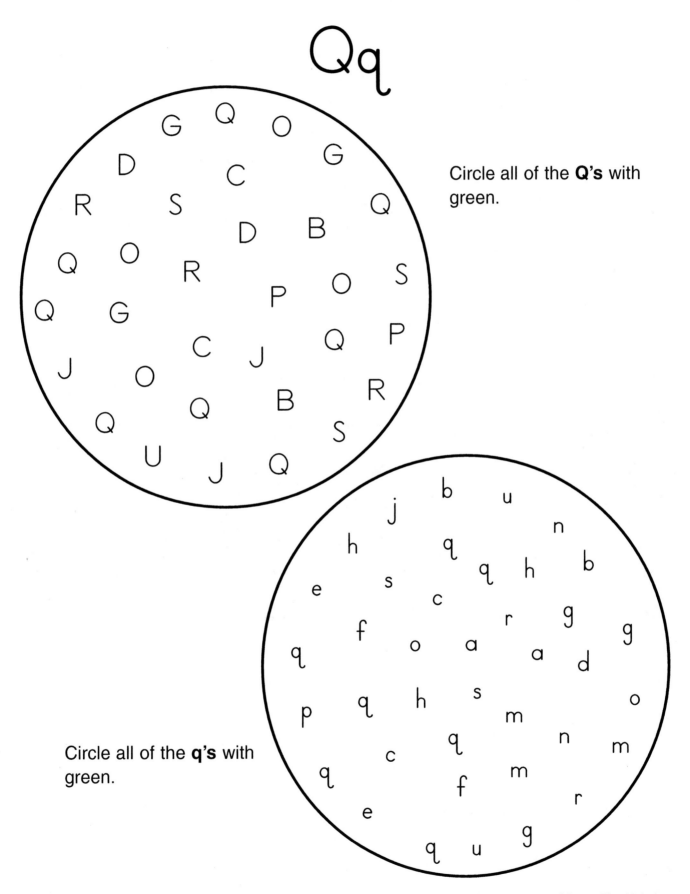

Circle all of the **Q's** with green.

Circle all of the **q's** with green.

Name: ______________________________

Color brown.

Q

q

Trace

Q Q Q

Trace

q q q q

Write

Q

Write

q

Draw a picture of something that begins with the sound of **Q**.

Color it brown.

Name: _____

_____

rake

Color

p – brown

q – red

r – green

Cut and glue on another piece of paper to make

Name: _____

Letter Search Bubbles

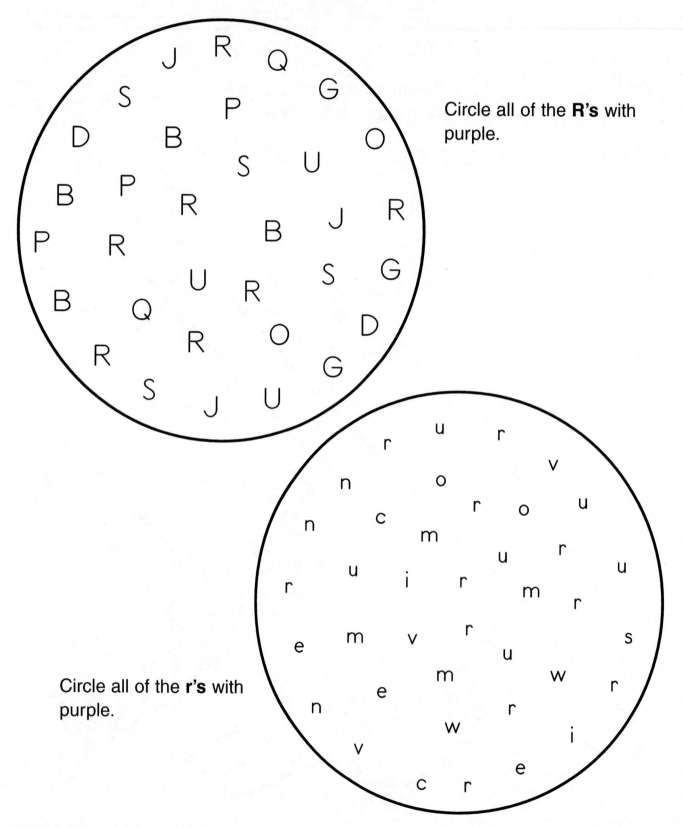

Circle all of the **R's** with purple.

Circle all of the **r's** with purple.

Name: ____________________

Color blue.

R

Trace

R R R

Trace

r

r r r r r

Write

R

Write

r

Draw a picture of something that begins with the sound of **R**.

Color it blue.

sign

Color

r – red

s – black

Cut and glue on
another piece of paper
to make

Name: _____

Letter Search Bubbles

Ss

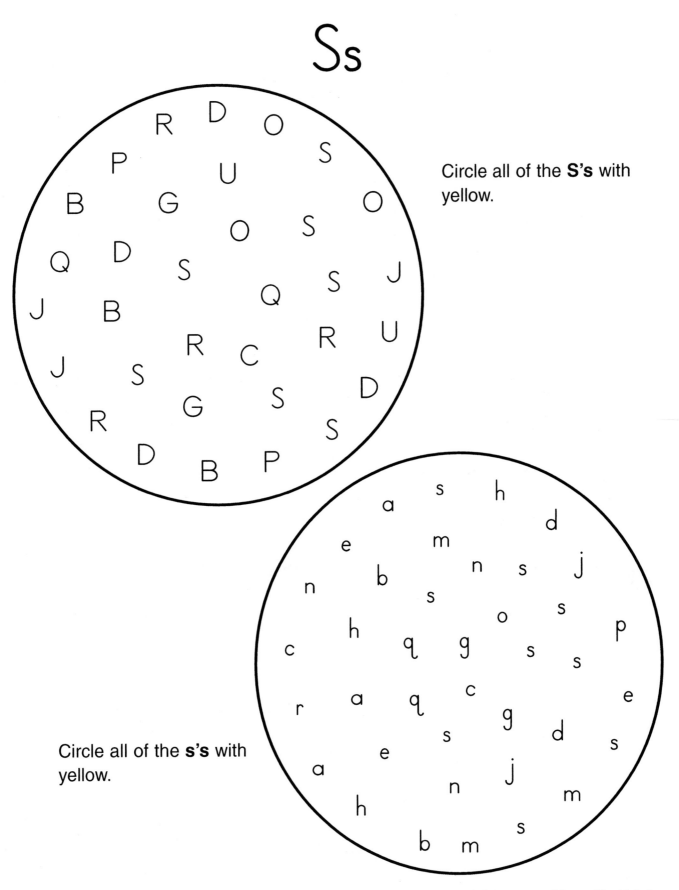

Circle all of the **S's** with yellow.

Circle all of the **s's** with yellow.

Name: _____

Color yellow.

S

Trace

S S S S

Trace

s

S S S S S

Write

S

Write

s

Draw a picture of something that begins with the sound of **S**.

Color it yellow.

Name: _____

top

Color

m – red

n – brown

o – yellow

p – blue

q – green

r – purple

s – orange

t – black

Cut and glue on another piece of paper to make

n

m

o

p

q

r

s

t

Letter Search Bubbles

T t

Circle all of the **T's** with black.

Circle all of the **t's** with black.

Name: _____

Color green.

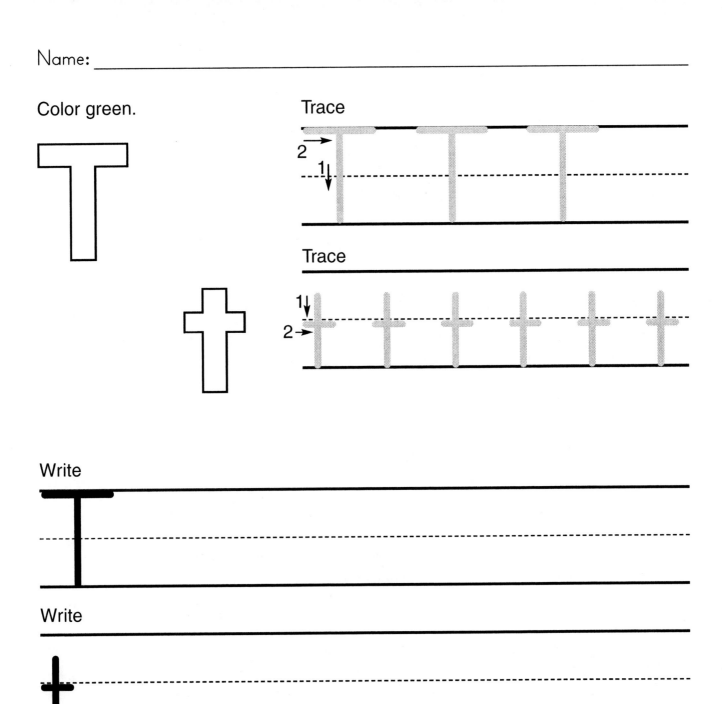

Trace

Trace

Write

Write

Draw a picture of something that begins with the sound of **T**.

Color it green.

Name: _____

umbrella

Color

s – black

t – red

u – blue

Cut and glue on another piece of paper to make

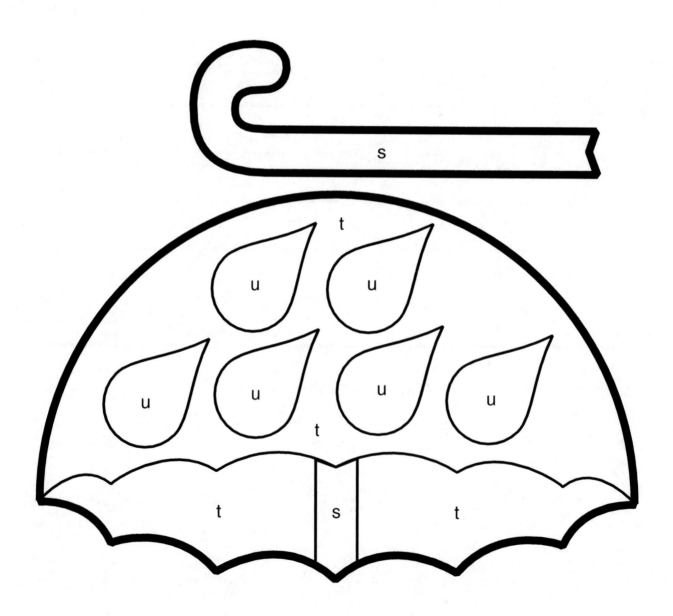

Letter Search Bubbles

Uu

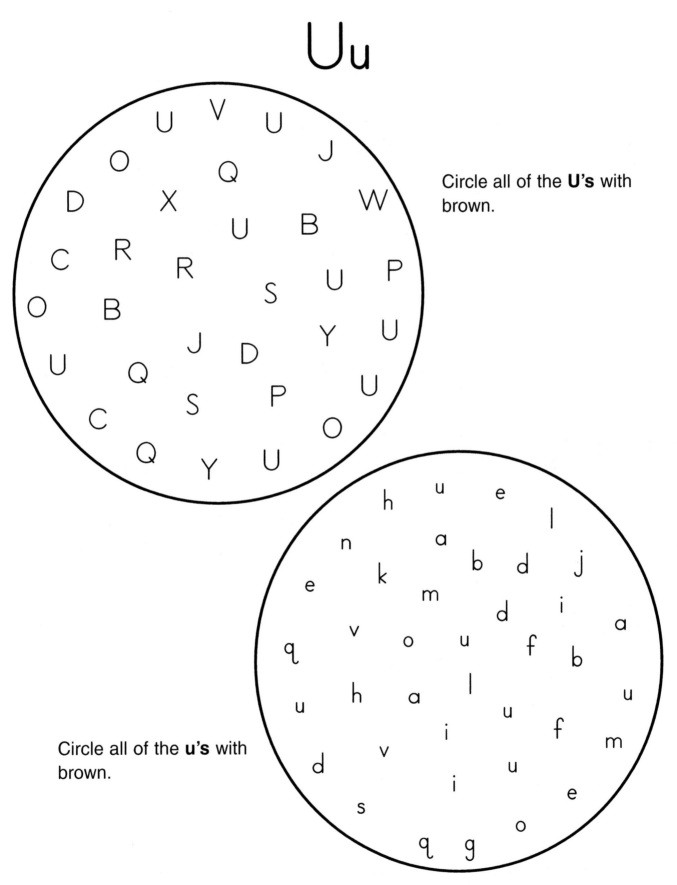

Circle all of the **U's** with brown.

Circle all of the **u's** with brown.

Color orange.

Trace

1↓

Trace

1↓ ↓2

Write

Write

Draw a picture of something that begins with the sound of **U**.

Color it orange.

Name: _____

valentine

Color

u – black

v – red

Cut and glue on another
piece of paper to make

Name: _____

Letter Search Bubbles

Vv

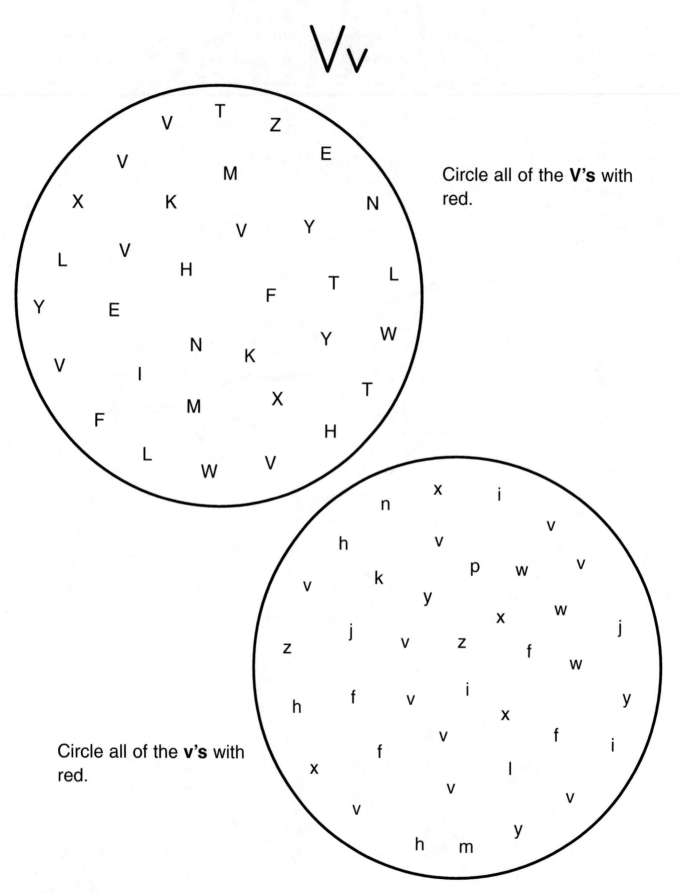

Circle all of the **V's** with red.

Circle all of the **v's** with red.

Name: _____

Color purple.

Trace

1 \ / 2 VVVV

Trace

1 \ / 2 VVVV

Write

V

Write

V

Draw a picture of something that begins with the sound of **V**.

Color it purple.

windmill

Color

u – green

v – orange

w – brown

Cut and glue on another piece of paper to make

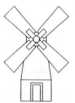

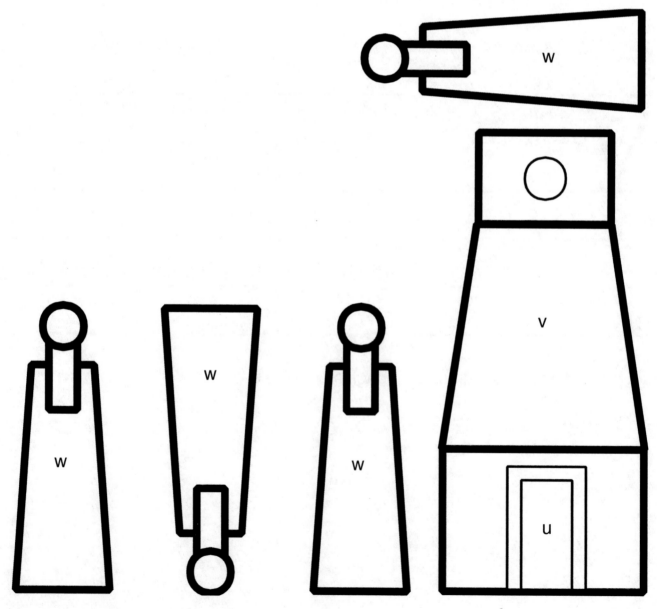

Letter Search Bubbles

Ww

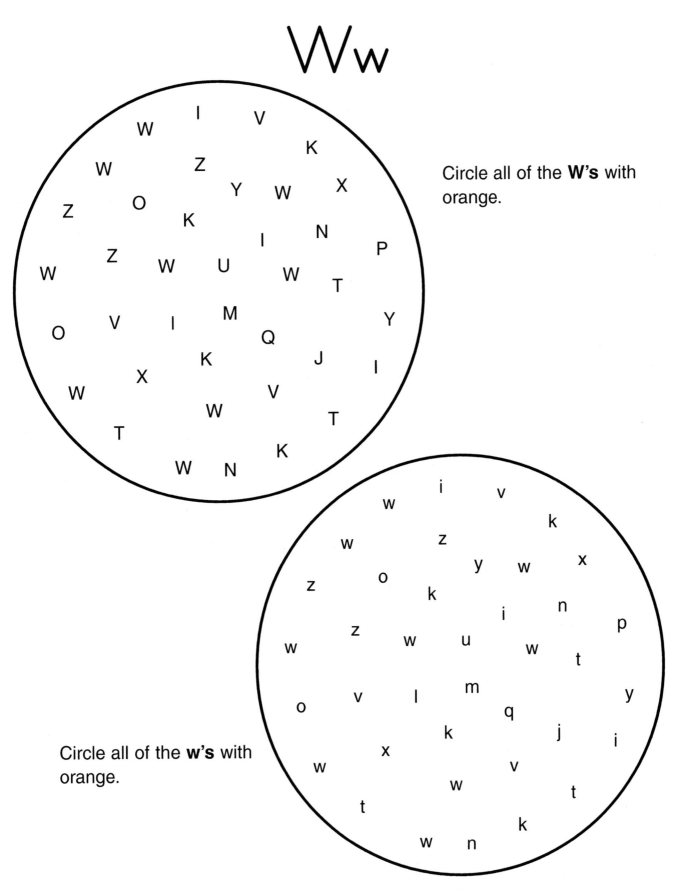

Circle all of the **W's** with orange.

Circle all of the **w's** with orange.

Name: _____

Color brown.

Trace

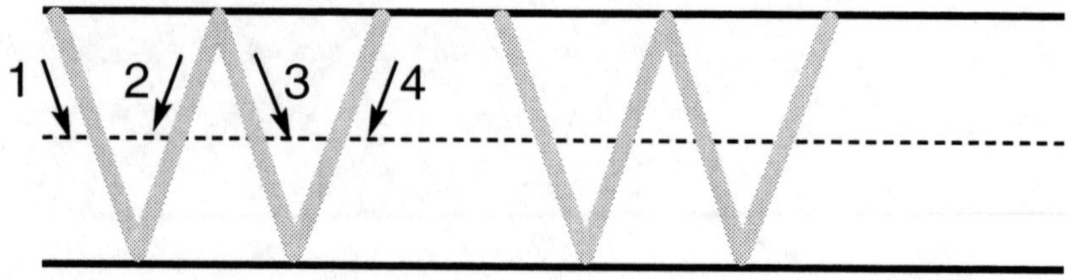

W

1 2 3 4

Trace

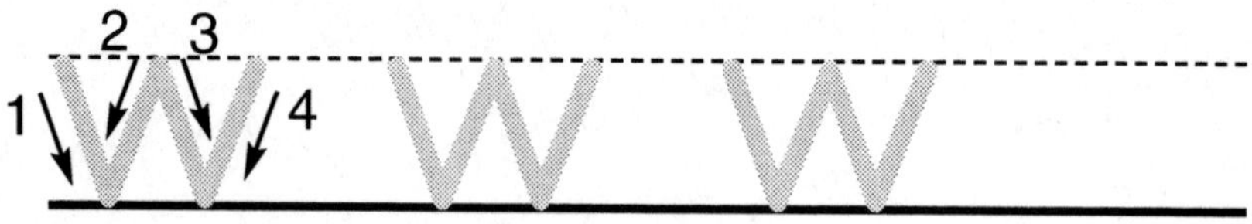

W

1 2 3 4

Write

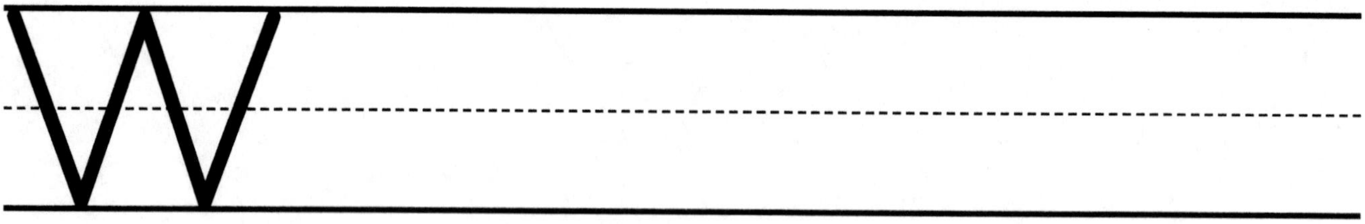

W

Write

W

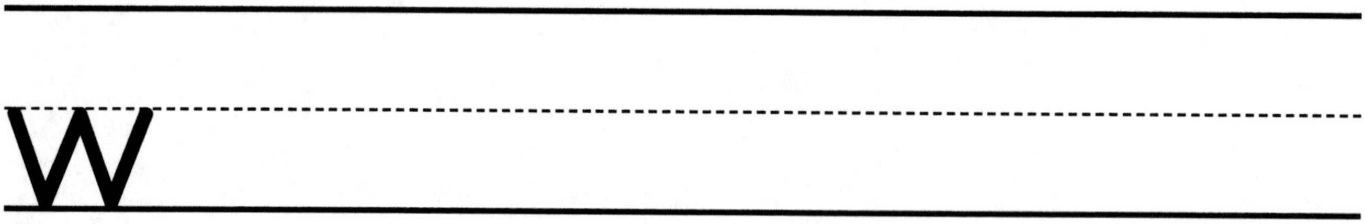

Draw a picture of something that begins with the sound of **W**.

Color it brown.

Name: _____

xylophone

Color

s – red

t – blue

u – yellow

v – green

w – purple

x – brown

Cut and glue on another piece of paper to make

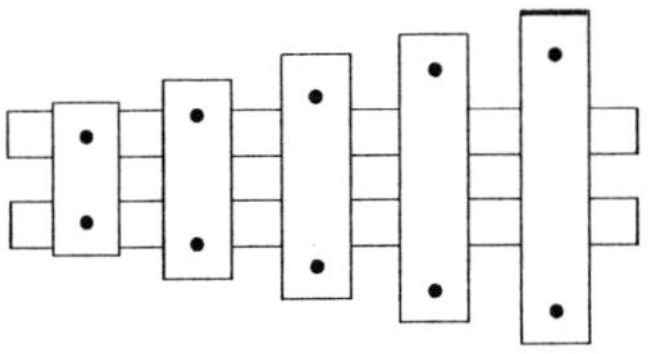

●   s   ●

●   t   ●

●   u   ●

●   v   ●

●   w   ●

x

x

Letter Search Bubbles

Xx

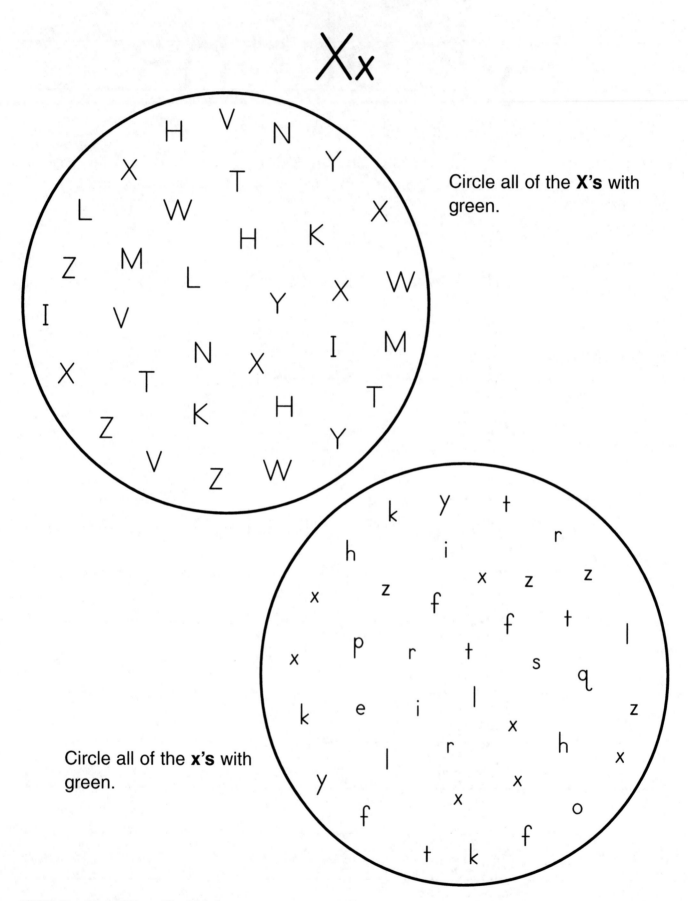

Circle all of the **X's** with green.

Circle all of the **x's** with green.

Name: _____

Color black.

X

Trace

1 \ / 2 X X X

Trace

x

1 \ / 2 X X X X

Write

X

Write

X

Draw a picture of something that begins with the sound of **X**.

Color it black.

Name: _____

----

yes

Color

y – purple

e – green

s – blue

Cut and glue on another
piece of paper to make

Add a yarn hanger.

YES

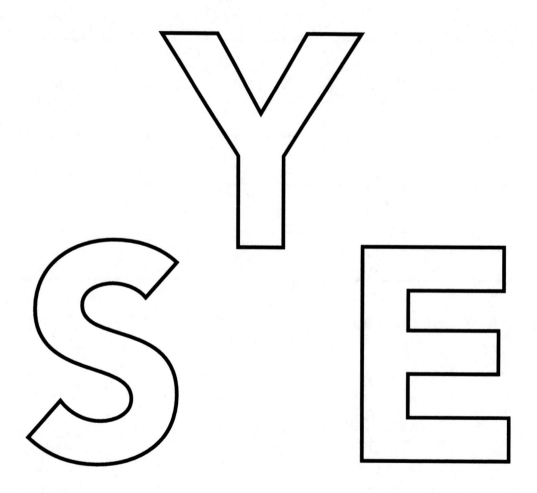

Letter Search Bubbles

Yy

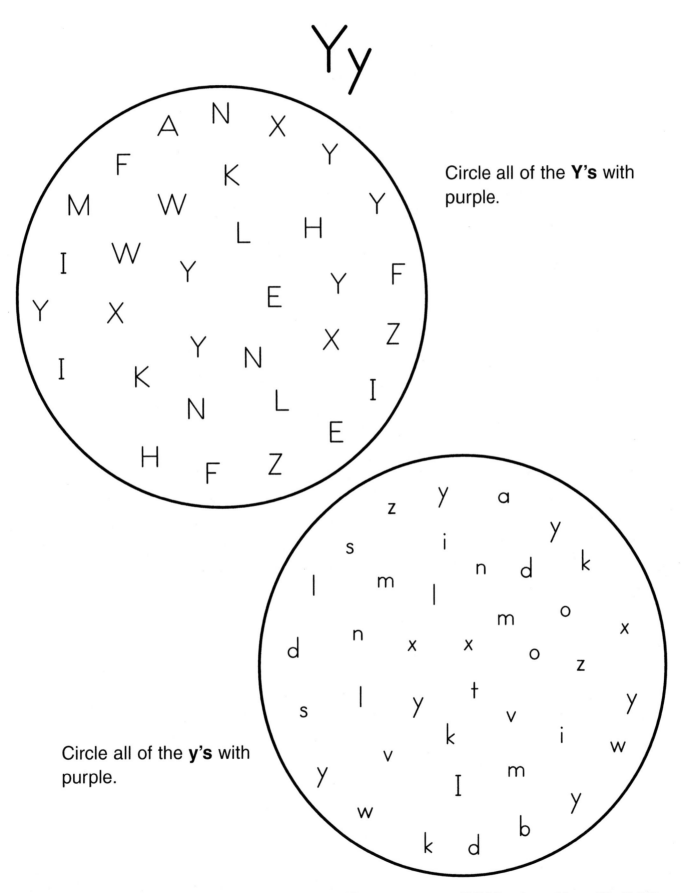

Circle all of the **Y's** with purple.

Circle all of the **y's** with purple.

Name: _____

Color red.

Y

Trace

1 ↘ Y ↙ 2   Y   Y   Y

Trace

1 ↘ y ↙ 2   y   y   y

y

Write

Y

Write

y

Draw a picture of something that begins with the sound of **Y**.

Color it red.

zip code

Color the zip code yellow. Write the price of the stamp.

Cut out the pieces and glue them in the correct places on the envelope.

From

To

Stamp
____ ¢

1 2 3 4 5

Letter Search Bubbles

Zz

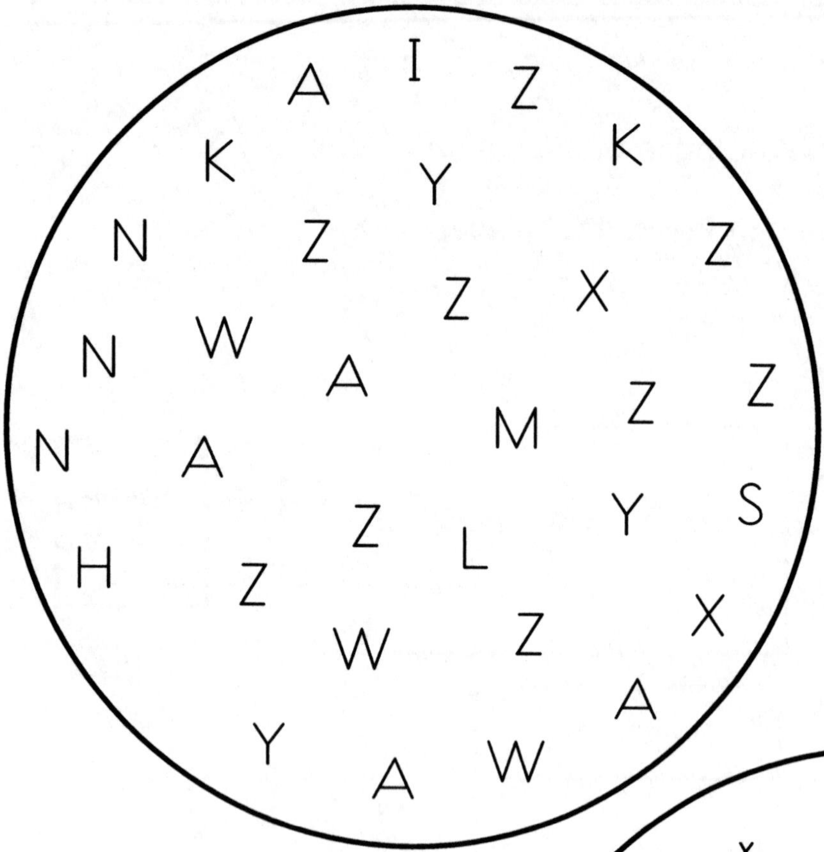

A I Z K
K Y
N Z K Z
N W Z X
A Z Z
N A M Z
Z Y S
H Z L X
W Z
Y A W A

Circle all of the **Z's** with blue.

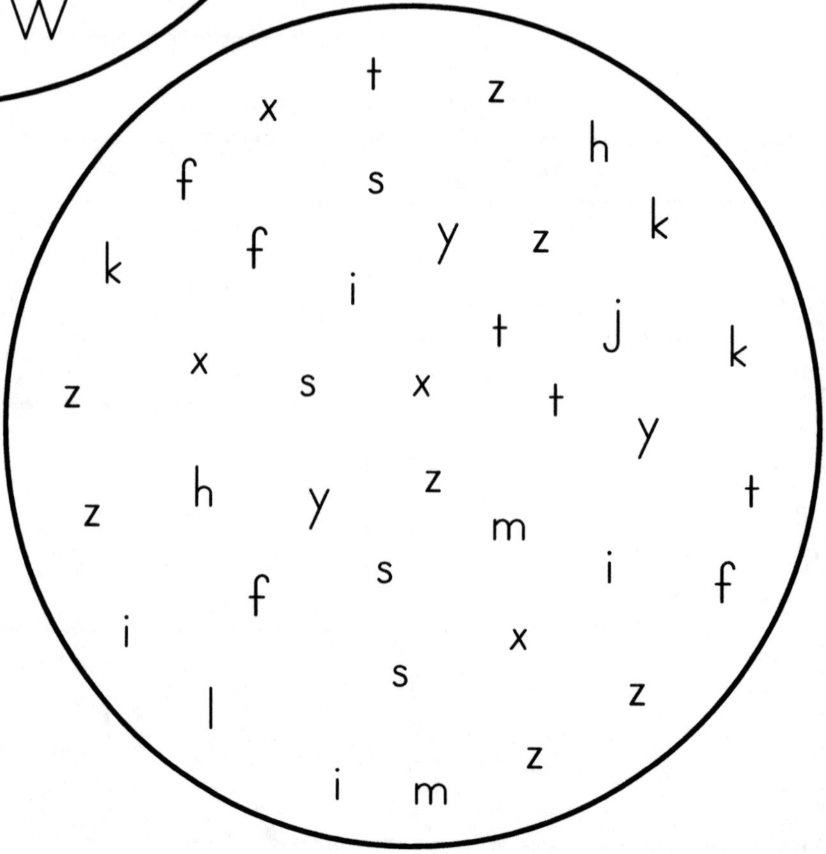

Circle all of the **z's** with blue.

x t z
f s h
k f y z k
i
x t j k
z s x t
y
z h y z t
m
f s i f
i x
s z
l z
i m

Name: _____

Color blue.

Z

Trace

1 → Z 2
3 →
Z Z

Trace

Z

1 → Z 2
3
Z Z Z Z

Write

Z _____

Write

Z _____

Draw a picture of something that begins with the sound of **Z**.

Color it blue.

Alphabet Little Books

Alphabet Autographs

Teacher Directions: Use this cover with pages 124–136 to have the children create autograph books. First, have them cut out the pages. Help them to arrange their pages in alphabetical order. Staple the pages together into a book. Encourage the children to ask friends and relatives to sign the book. Each person should sign on the page bearing the first letter of his or her name.

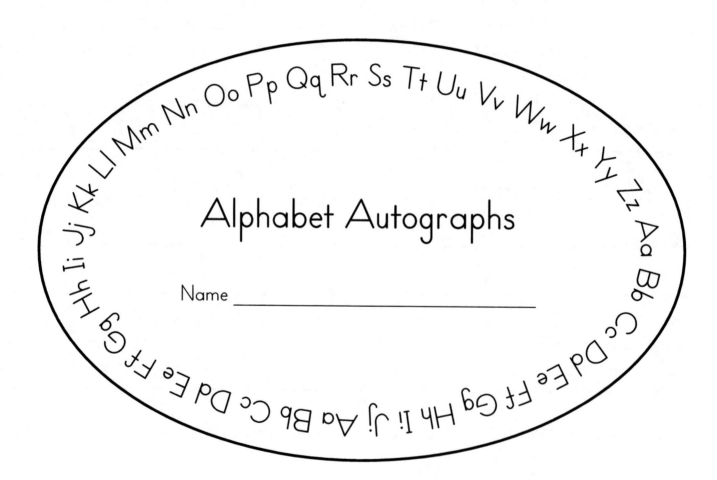

Alphabet Little Books *(cont.)*

Alphabet Dictionary

Teacher Directions: Use this cover with pages 124–136 to have the children create dictionaries. First have them cut out the pages. Help them to arrange their pages in alphabetical order. Staple the pages together into a book. Encourage the children to fill their dictionaries with words they see around them, such as "exit," "milk," "stop," etc. The students may also wish to add stickers or glue pictures to appropriate pages, such as adding a cat picture to page **C** or a doll picture to page **D**.

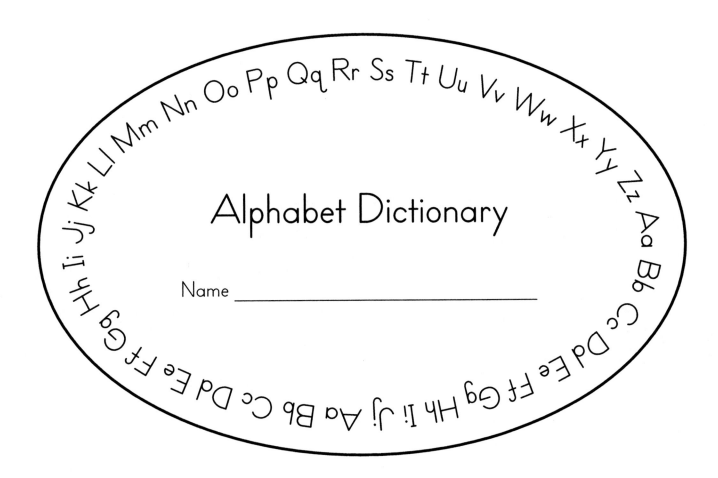

Alphabet Little Books (cont.)

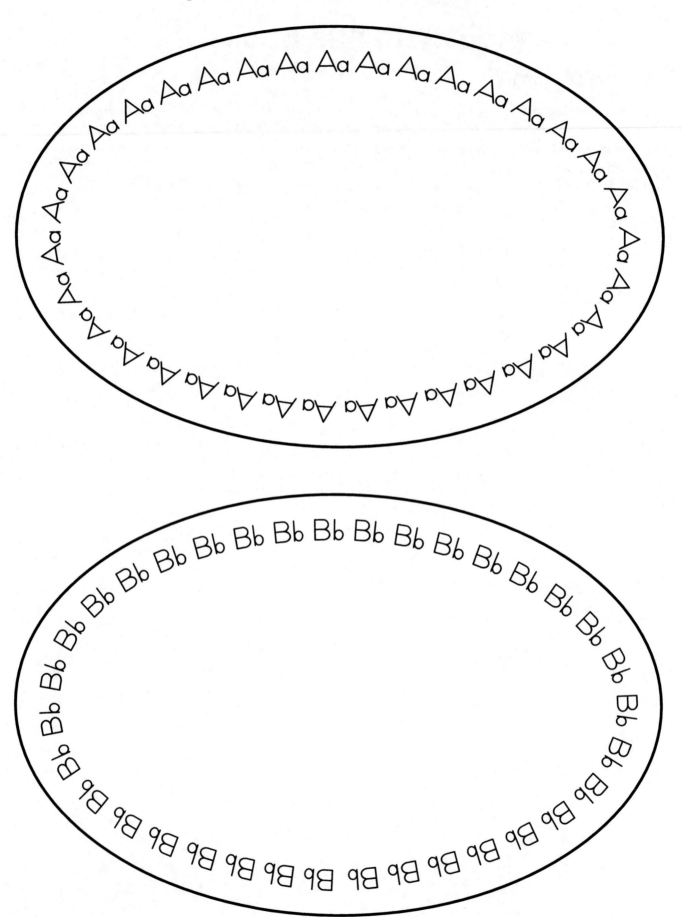

Alphabet Little Books (cont.)

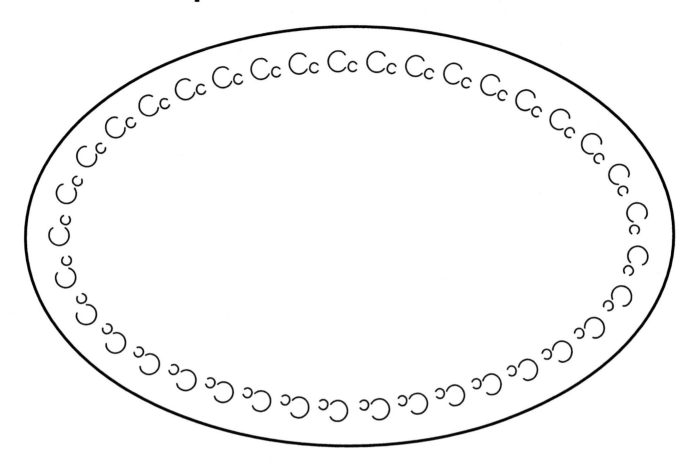

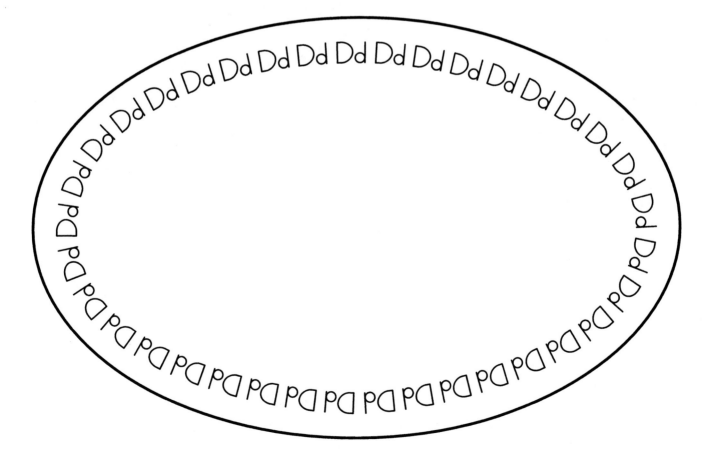

Alphabet Little Books (cont.)

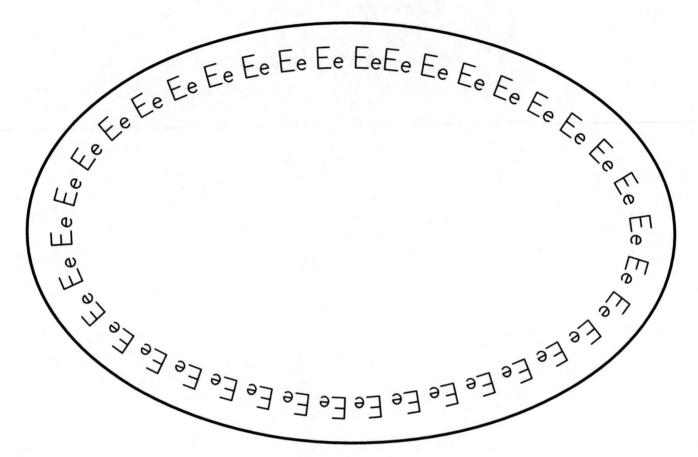

Alphabet Little Books *(cont.)*

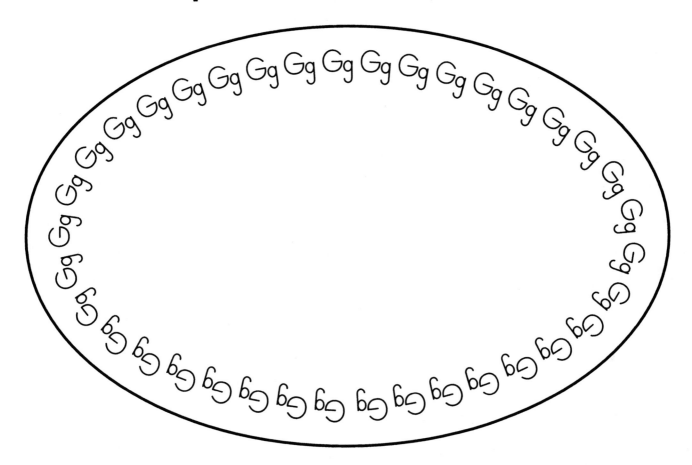

Alphabet Little Books *(cont.)*

Alphabet Little Books (cont.)

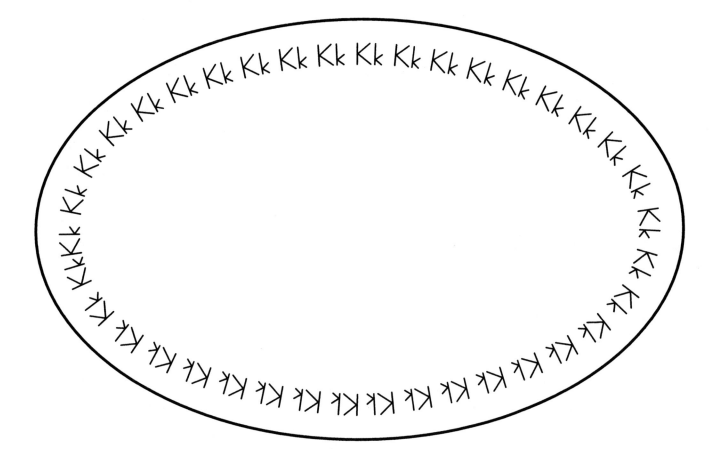

Alphabet Little Books (cont.)

Mm Mm Mm Mm Mm Mm Mm Mm Mm Mm Mm Mm Mm Mm Mm Mm Mm Mm Mm Mm Mm Mm Mm Mm Mm Mm Mm Mm Mm

Nn Nn Nn Nn Nn Nn Nn Nn Nn Nn Nn Nn Nn Nn Nn Nn Nn Nn Nn Nn Nn Nn Nn Nn Nn Nn Nn Nn Nn Nn Nn Nn

Alphabet Little Books *(cont.)*

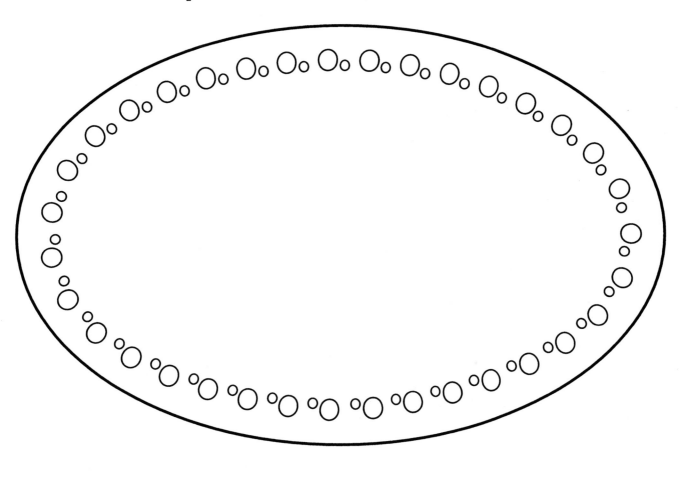

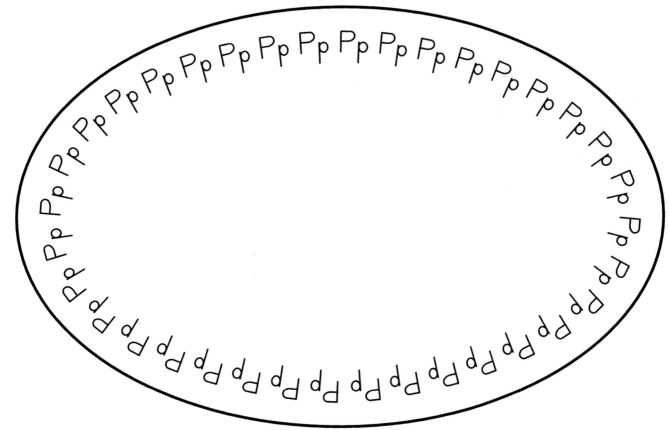

Alphabet Little Books (cont.)

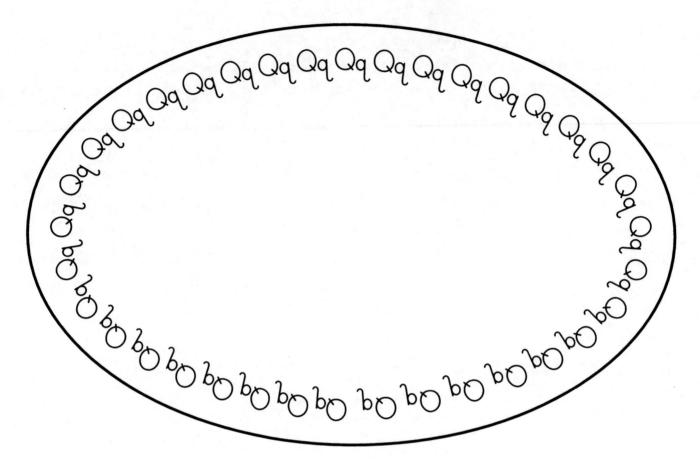

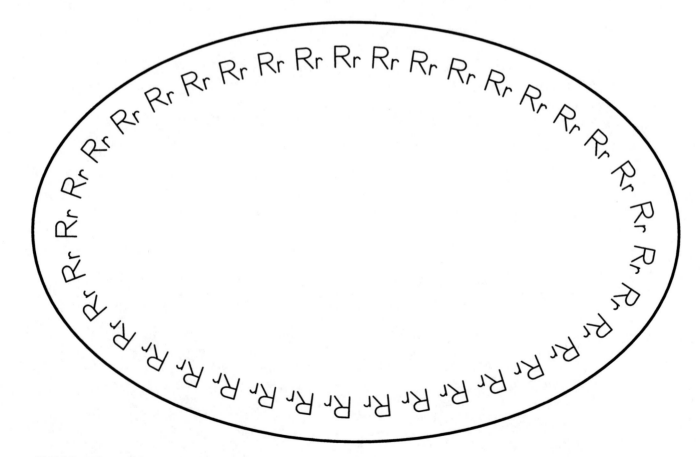

Alphabet Little Books *(cont.)*

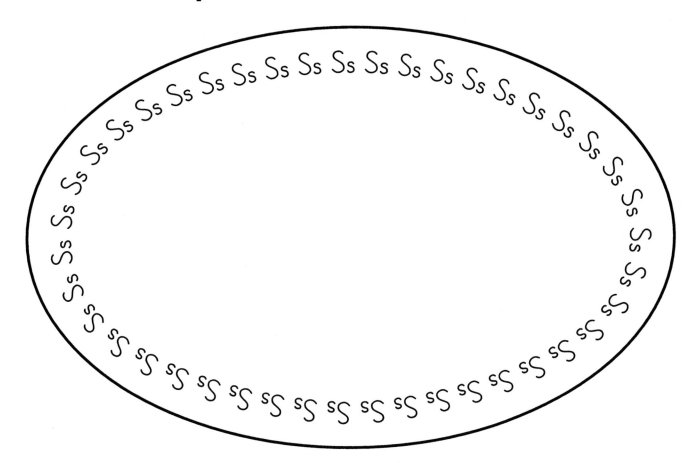

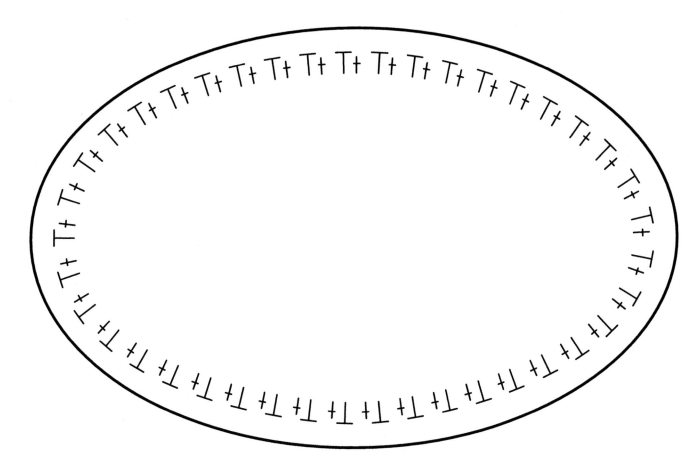

Alphabet Little Books (cont.)

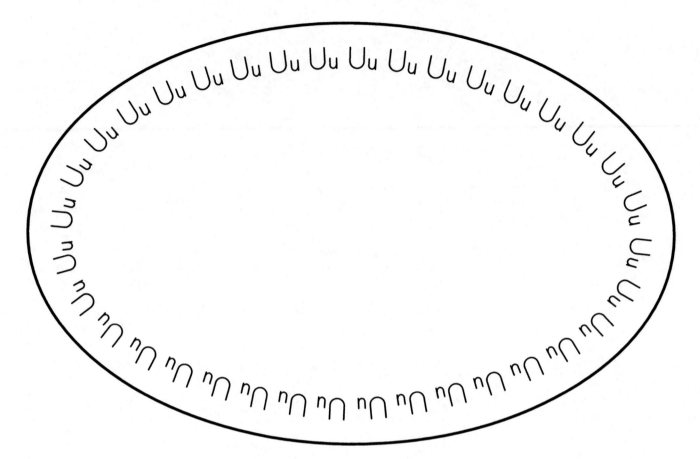

Alphabet Little Books *(cont.)*

Alphabet Little Books *(cont.)*

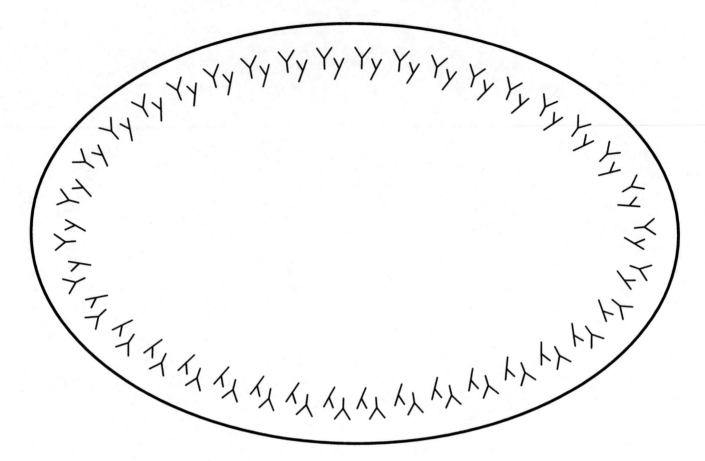

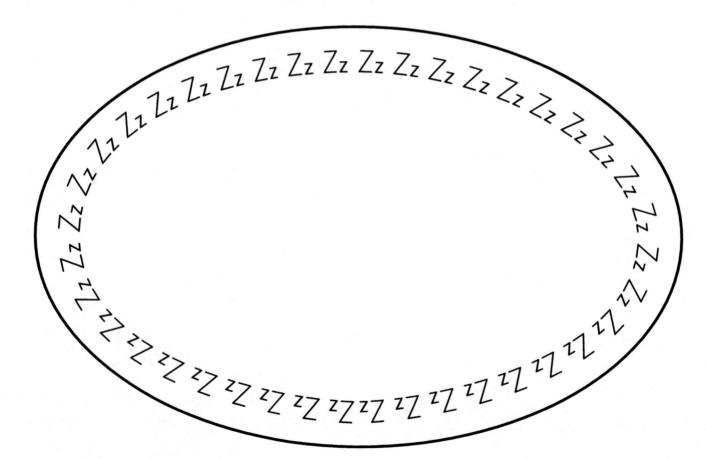

My Little Book of Colors

Teacher Directions: Use this cover with pages 138–141 to have each child create a book of colors. Help the students read the title of their little book. Let them write their names where indicated. On each page, the students are to identify the color word and color the picture. To complete the page, have the students cut as indicated by broken lines, then glue the letters into the boxes to spell the color word.

My Little Book of Colors

Name _____

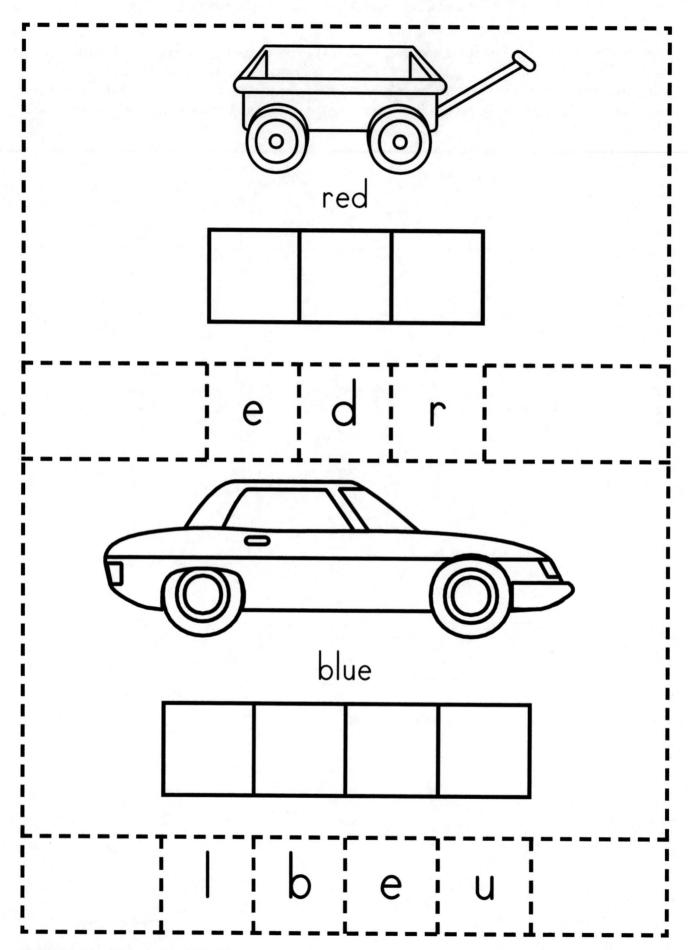

red

blue

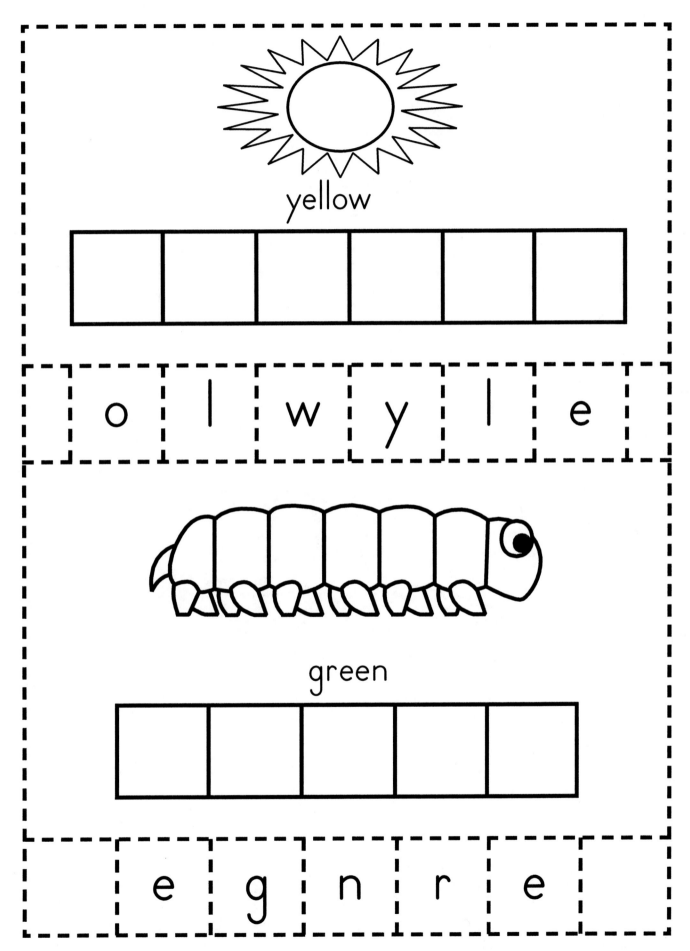

yellow

o l w y l e

green

e g n r e

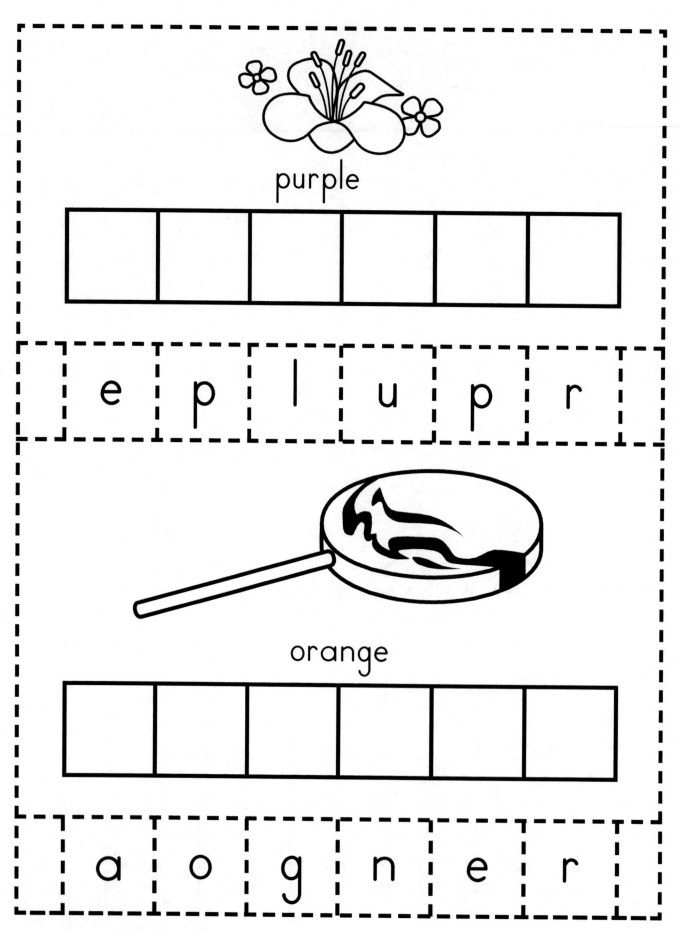

purple

e	p	l	u	p	r

orange

a	o	g	n	e	r

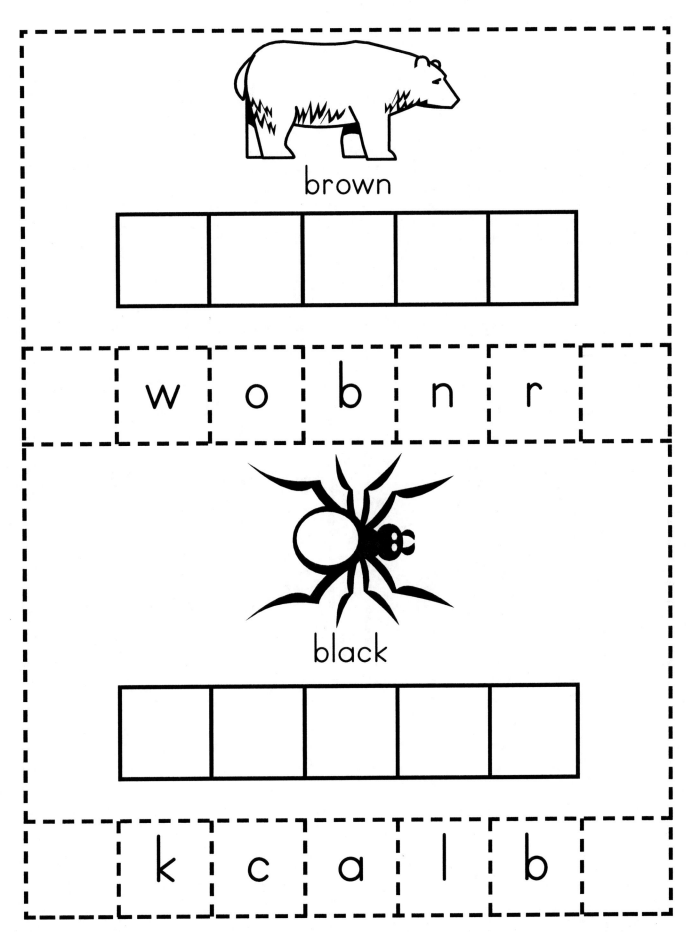

brown

w o b n r

black

k c a l b

Letter Pockets

Teacher Directions: Reproduce pages 142–148. Cut out the pocket shapes. Glue the pockets to one or more sheets of poster board in alphabetical order, leaving the top of each pocket open. Reproduce the Letter Pocket Cards on page 149.

Project 1—Challenge individual students to match upper- and lowercase letters by sliding each lowercase letter card into the appropriate pocket.

Project 2—Using the pocket card board(s) from Project 1, along with alphabet sound cards from a commercially produced set or pictures you cut from magazines, challenge the students to match the letters with their sounds by placing the pictures in appropriate pockets.

Project 3—Use masking tape to outline a large shirt shape on the floor of your classroom. Challenge the students to place the pockets on the shirt in alphabetical order.

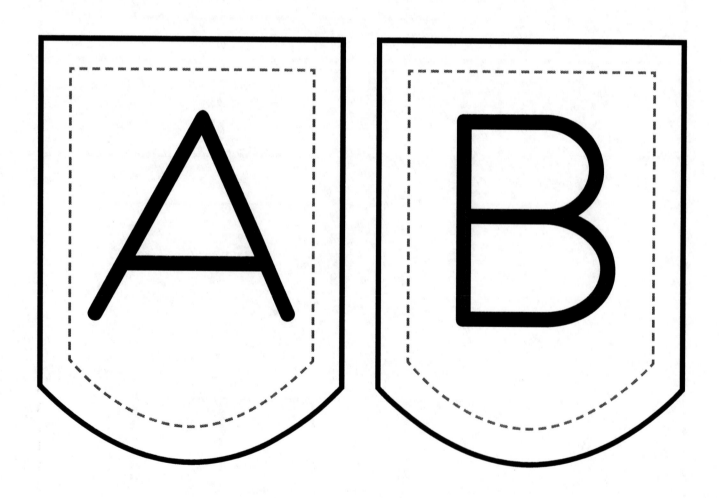

Letter Pockets *(cont.)*

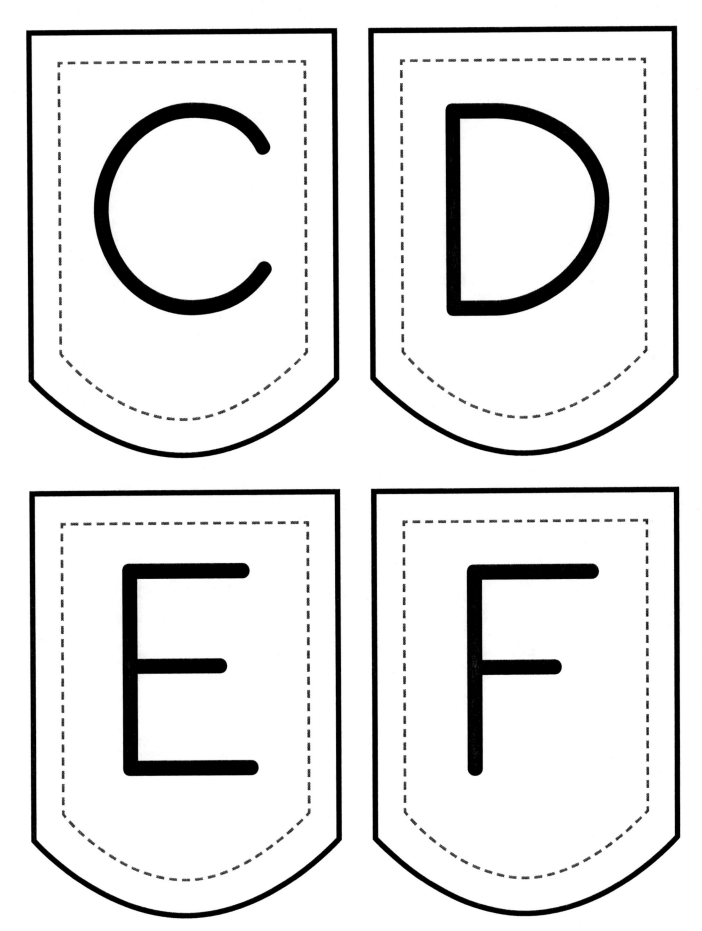

Letter Pockets *(cont.)*

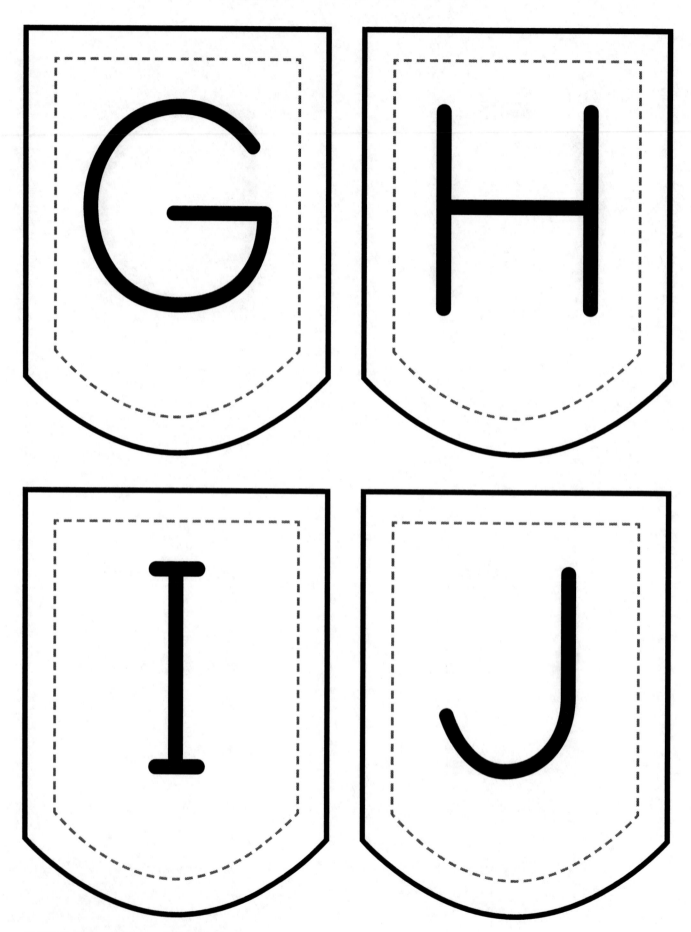

Letter Pockets *(cont.)*

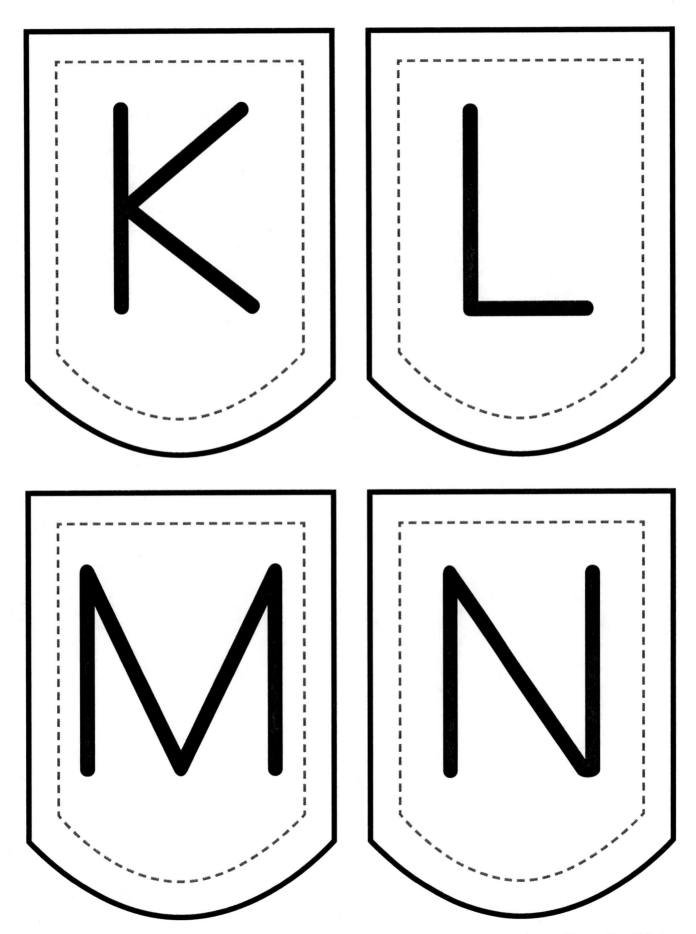

Letter Pockets *(cont.)*

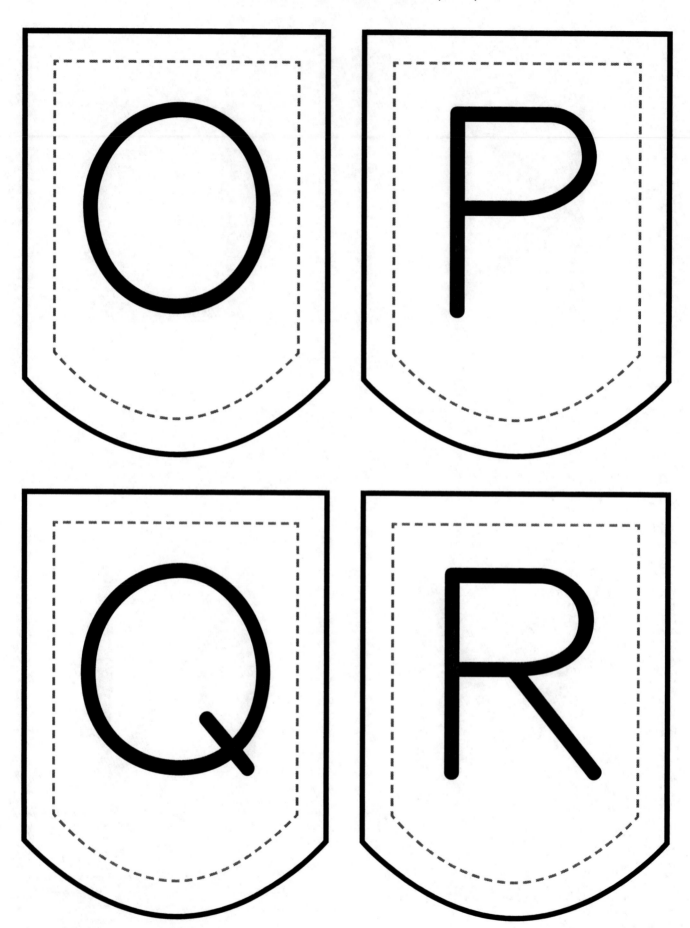

Letter Pockets *(cont.)*

Letter Pockets *(cont.)*

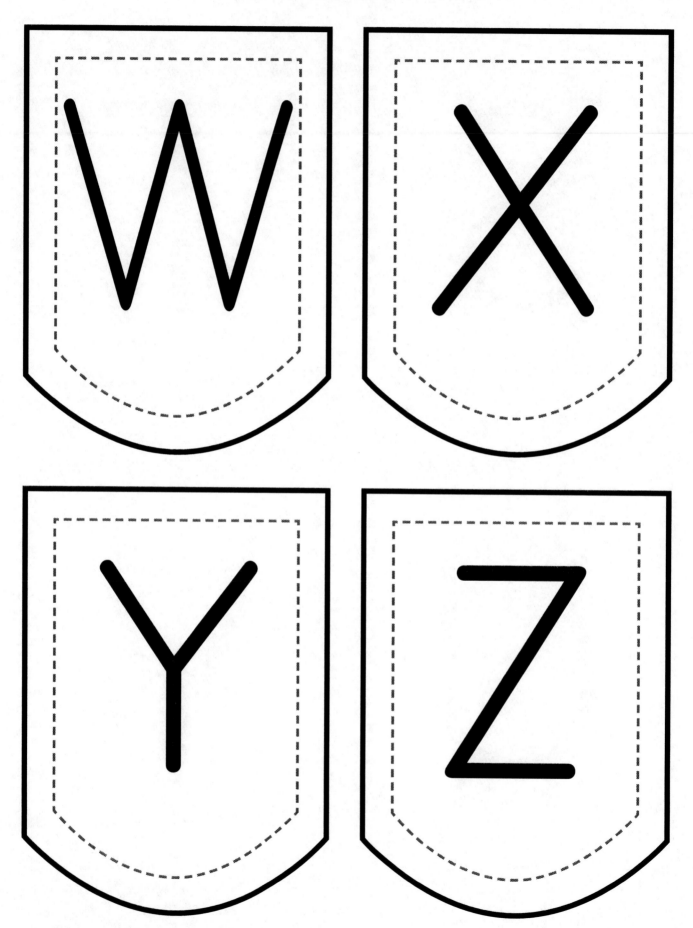

Letter Pocket Cards

Teacher Directions: Reproduce this page and invite the students to cut the cards apart. Use the cards with the activities listed on page 142.

		a	b
c	d	e	f
g	h	i	j
k	l	m	n
o	p	q	r
s	t	u	v
w	x	y	z

Lotto Cards

Teacher Directions: Use these cards on pages 150–153 with the Letter Match Lotto project, as directed on page 16. You will also need a copy of the Letter Pocket Cards on page 149.

I	P	A
V	D	M
S	Y	E

Lotto Cards (cont.)

D	G	Z
F	Q	A
J	U	H

Lotto Cards *(cont.)*

I	L	C
W	F	T
G	B	N

Lotto Cards *(cont.)*

B	C	X
J	H	E
O	K	R

Party Lights

Teacher Directions:

1. Reproduce pages 154–167.

2. Let the children help color the party lights with markers.

3. Laminate the pages.

4. Cut out the lights.

5. Use the lights with the Party Lights activity on page 18.

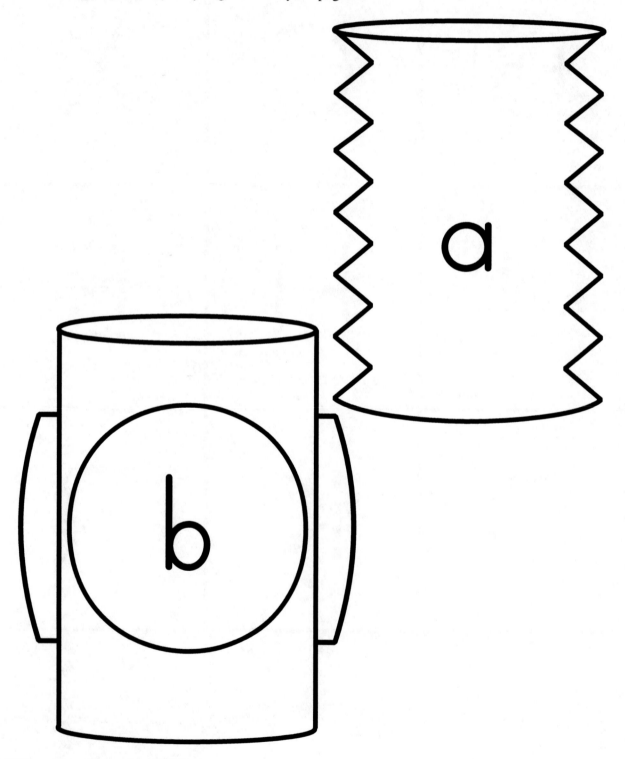

Party Lights *(cont.)*

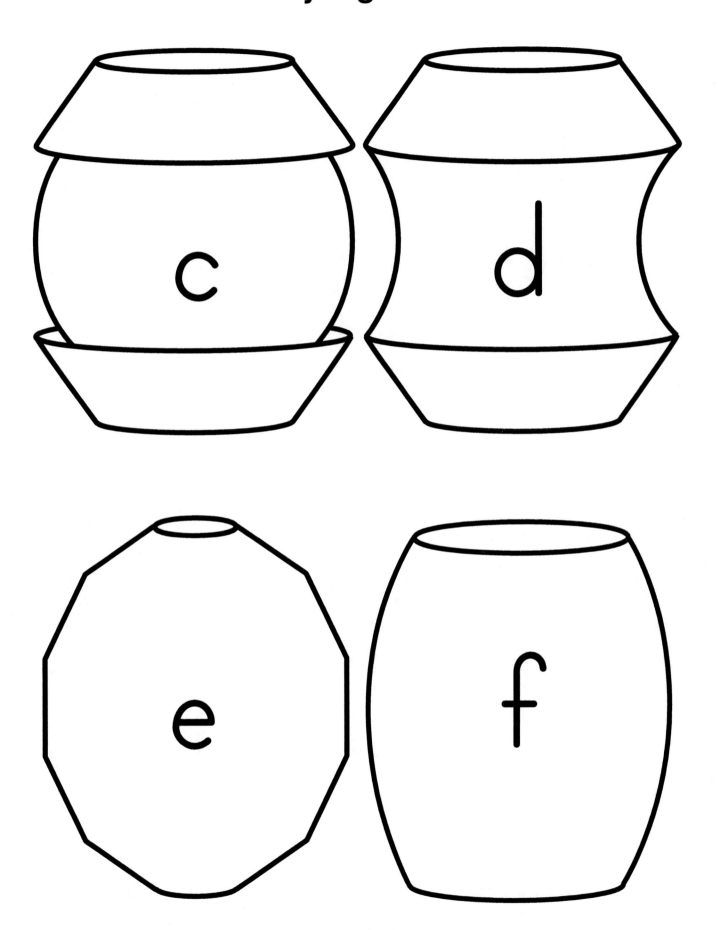

Party Lights *(cont.)*

Party Lights *(cont.)*

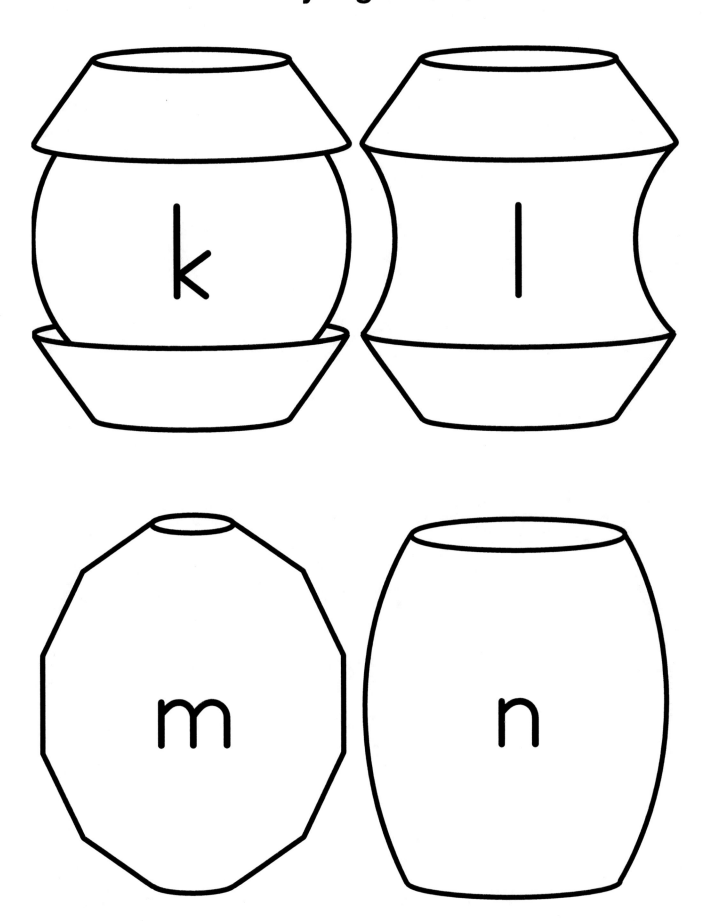

Party Lights *(cont.)*

Party Lights *(cont.)*

Party Lights *(cont.)*

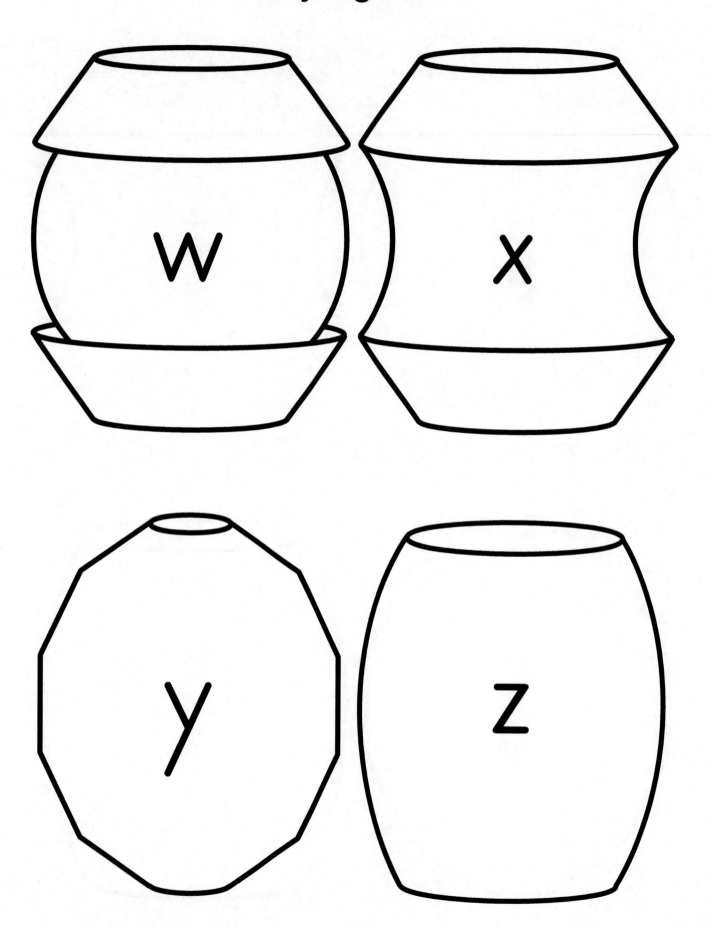

Party Lights *(cont.)*

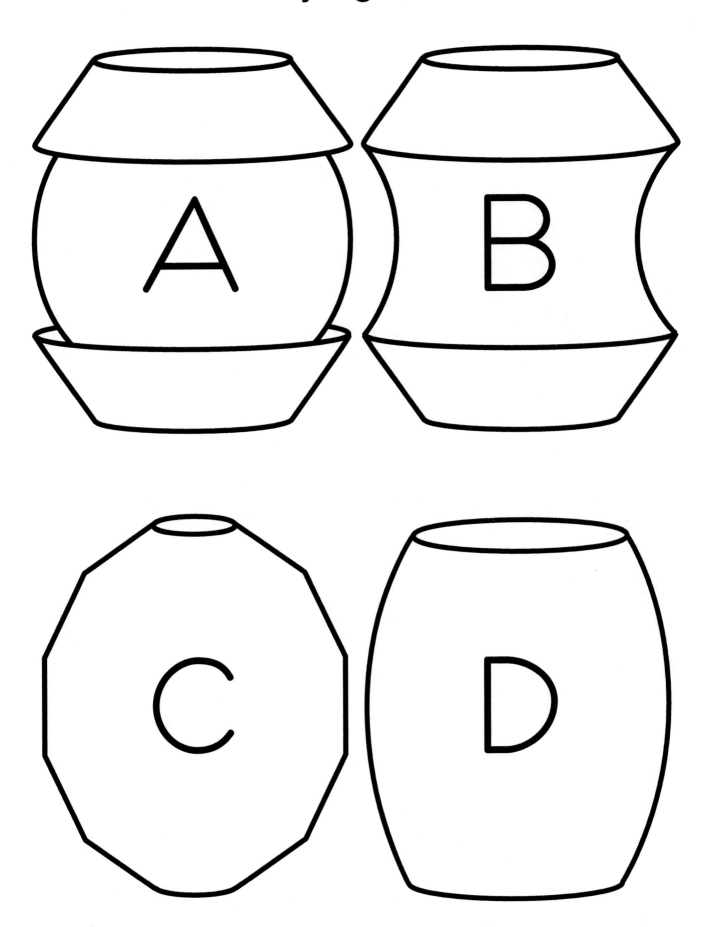

Party Lights *(cont.)*

Party Lights *(cont.)*

Party Lights *(cont.)*

Party Lights *(cont.)*

Party Lights *(cont.)*

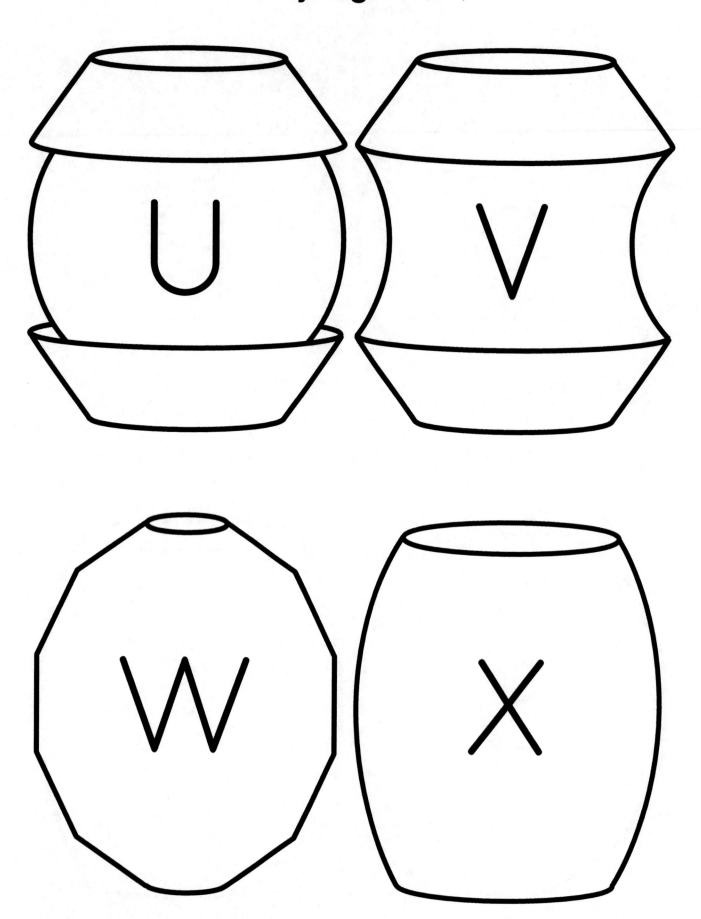

Party Lights *(cont.)*

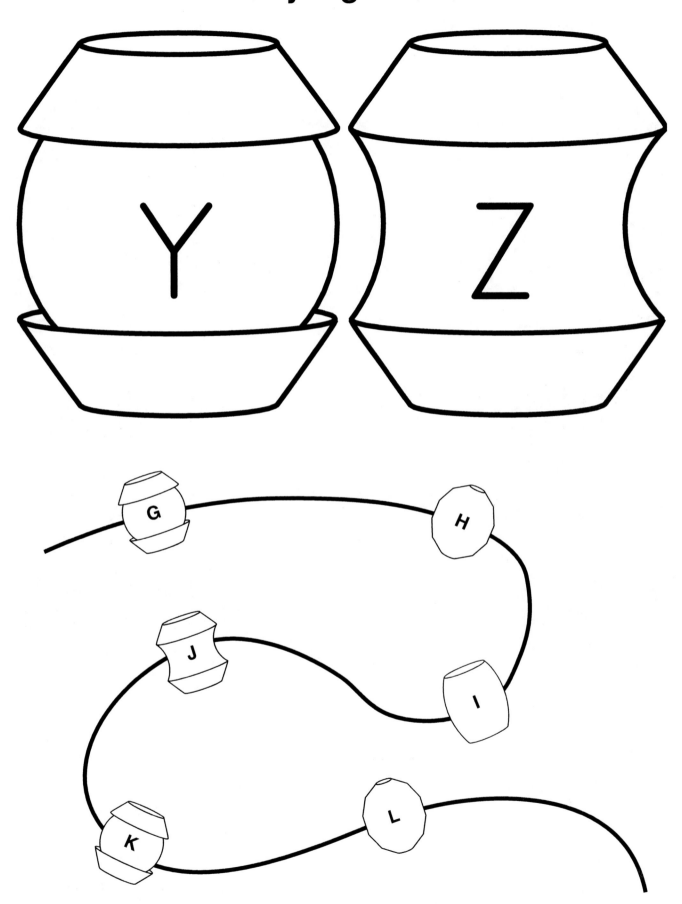

Mitten Match Cards

Teacher Directions: Reproduce pages 168–180 and have the students cut the cards apart. Use these cards with the Letter Pairs project, as directed on page 13.

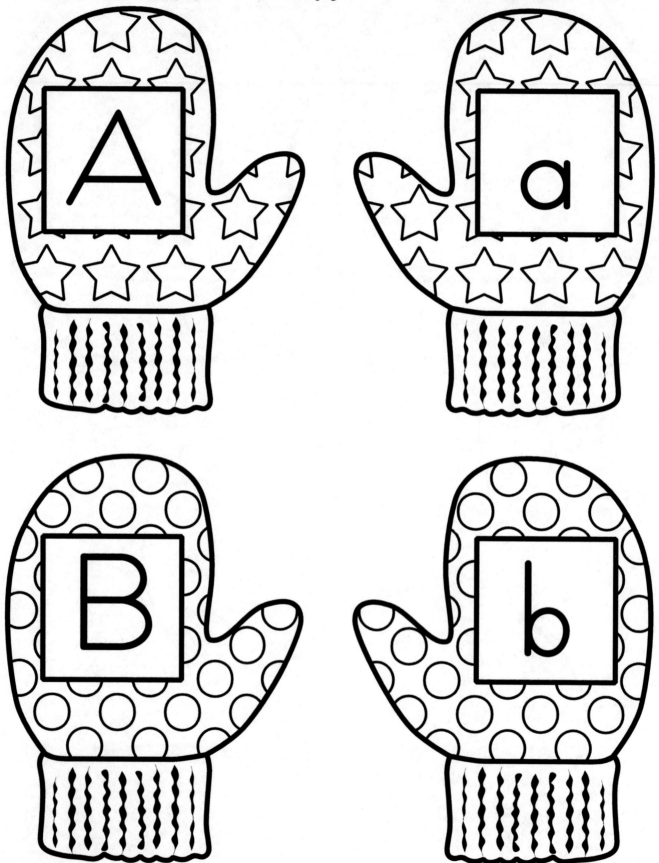

Mitten Match Cards *(cont.)*

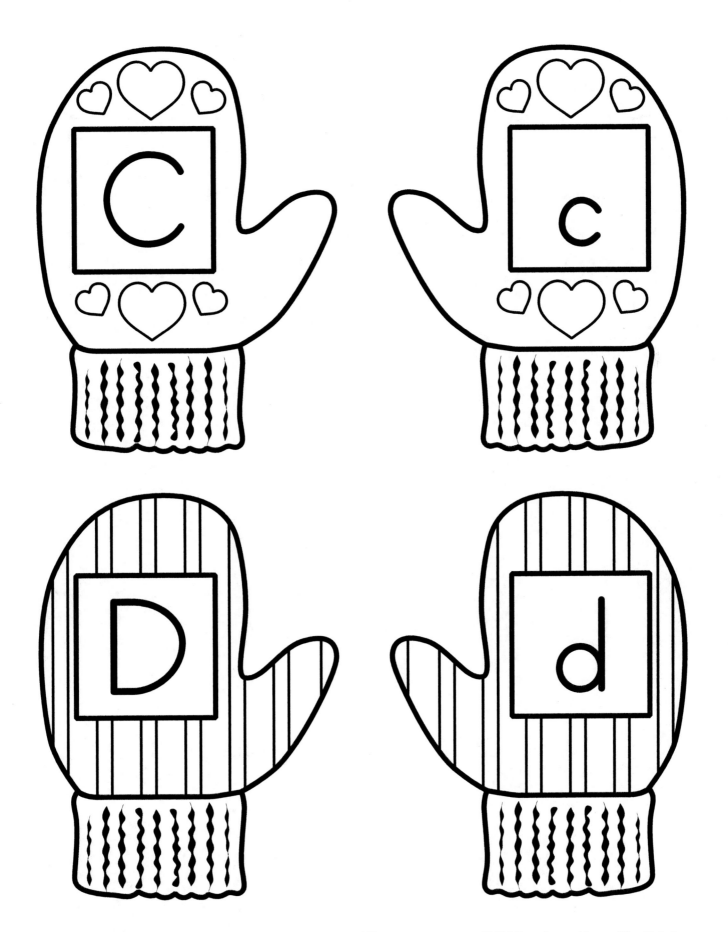

Mitten Match Cards *(cont.)*

Mitten Match Cards *(cont.)*

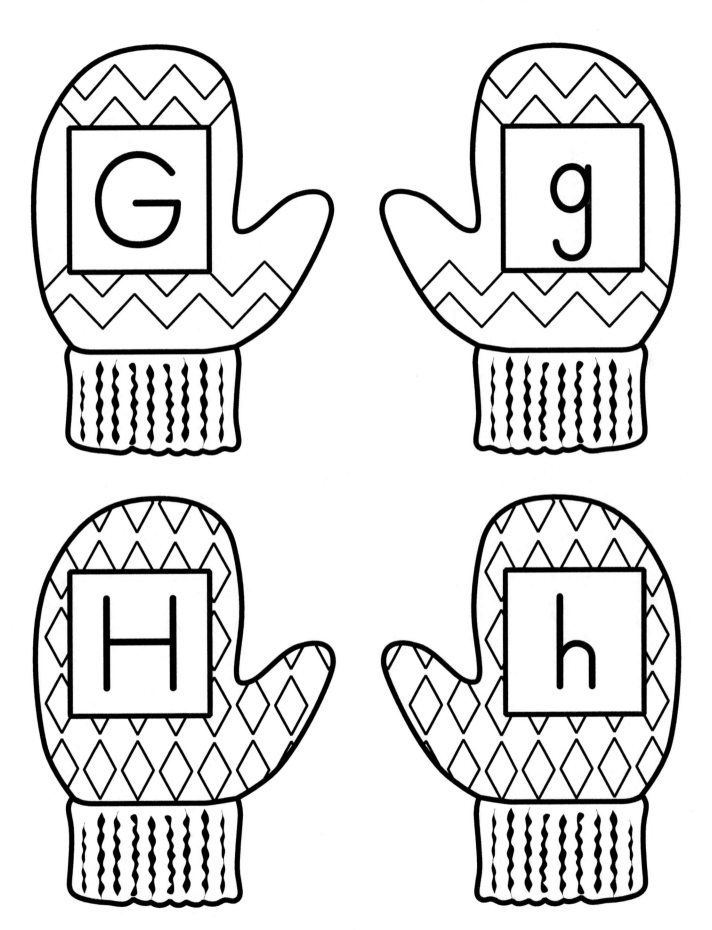

Mitten Match Cards *(cont.)*

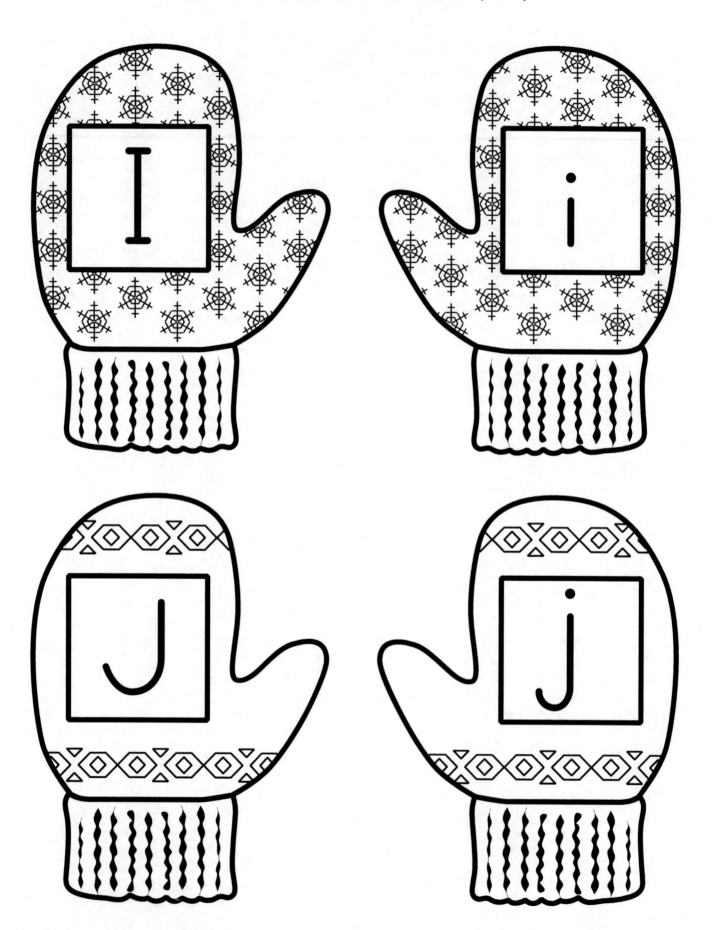

Mitten Match Cards *(cont.)*

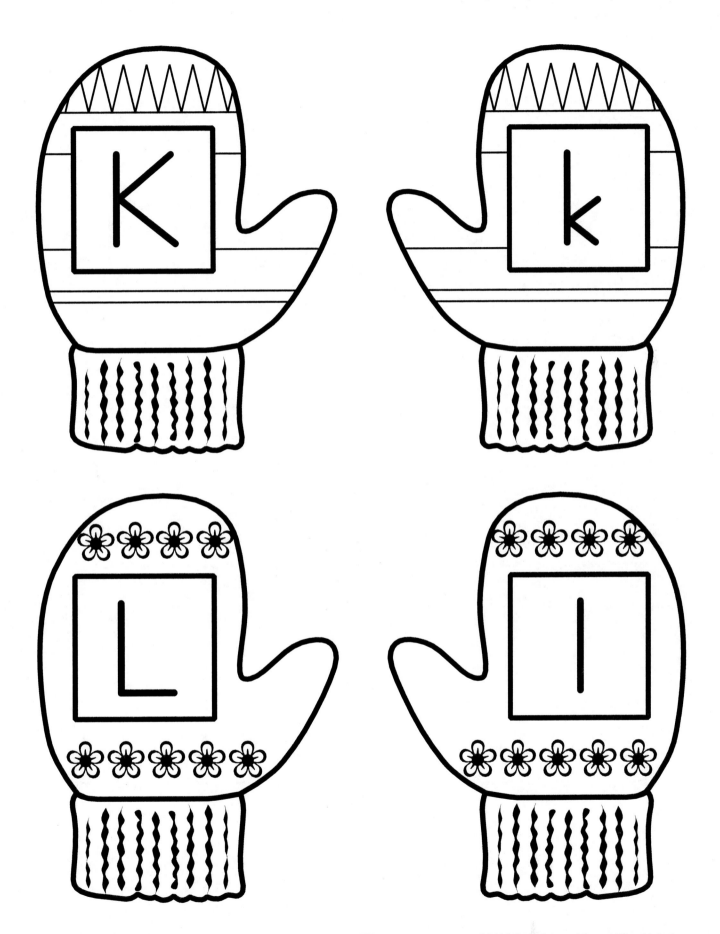

Mitten Match Cards *(cont.)*

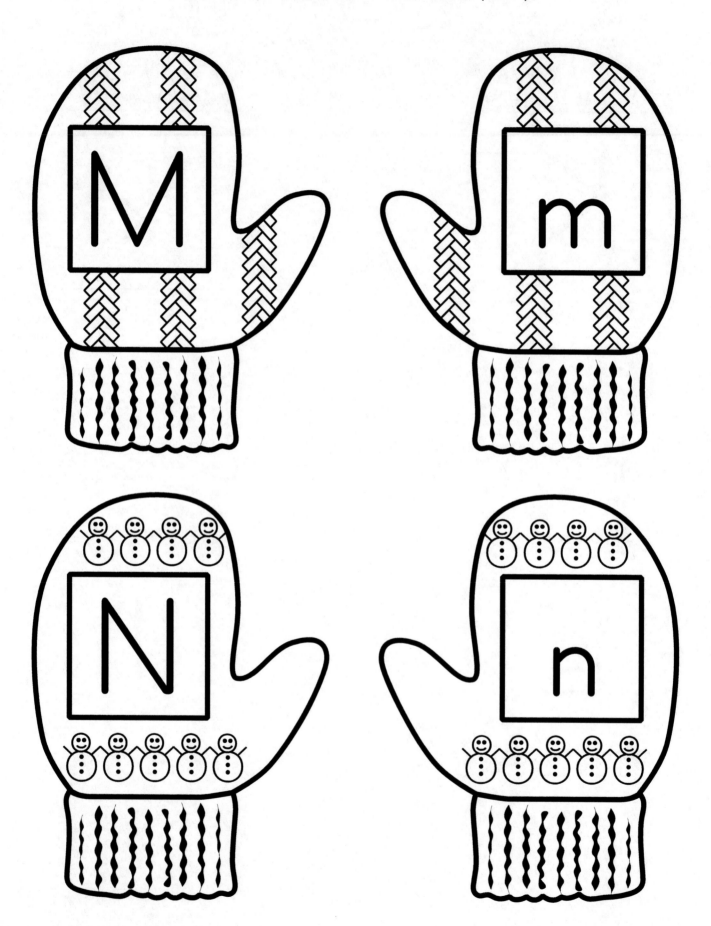

Mitten Match Cards *(cont.)*

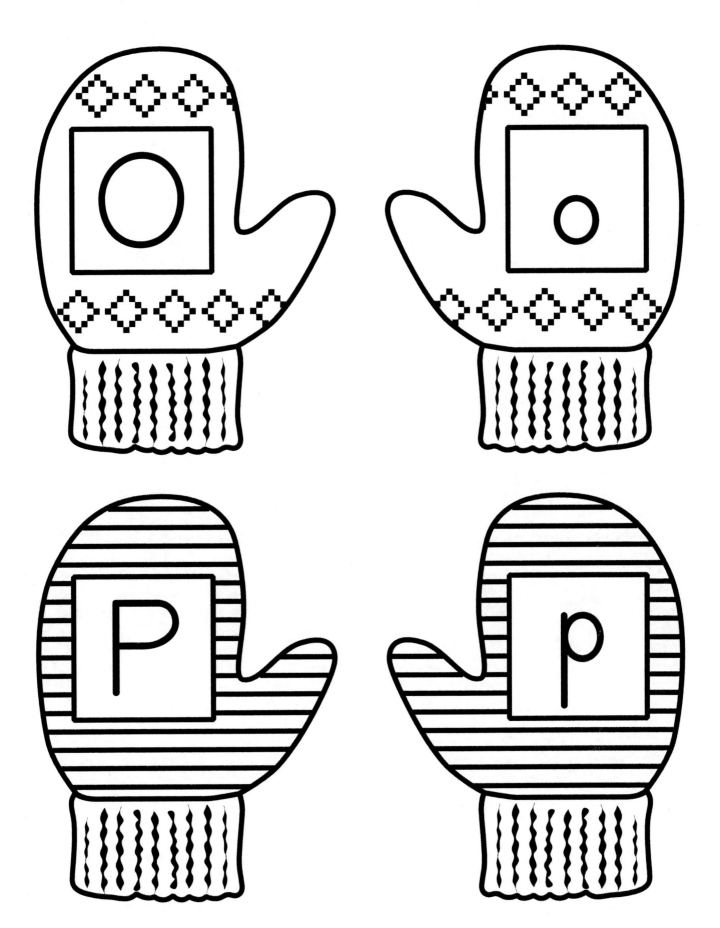

Mitten Match Cards *(cont.)*

Mitten Match Cards *(cont.)*

Mitten Match Cards *(cont.)*

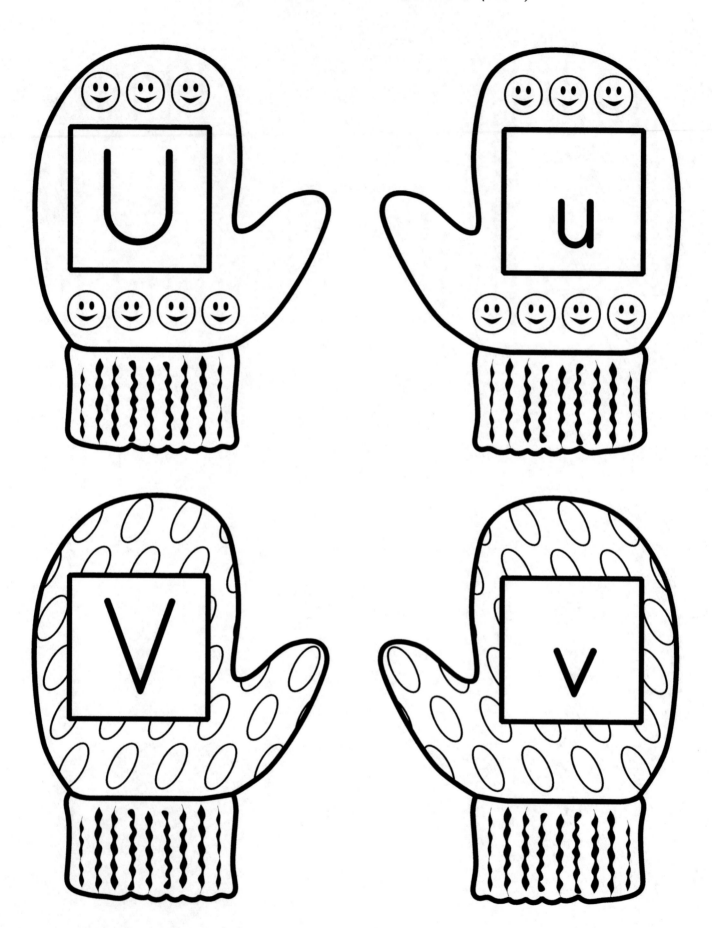

Mitten Match Cards *(cont.)*

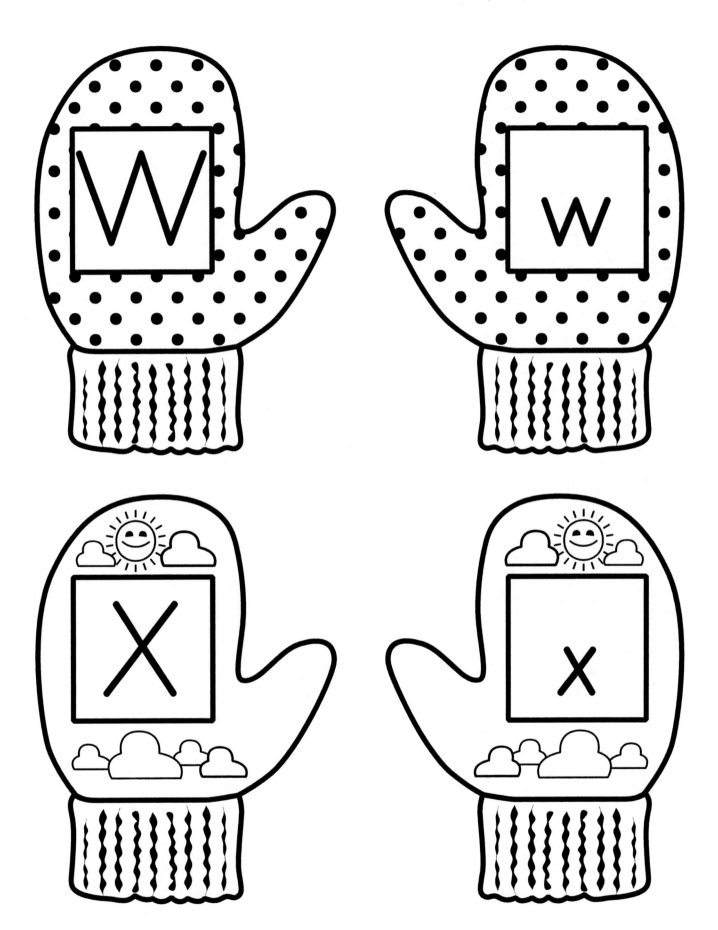

Mitten Match Cards *(cont.)*

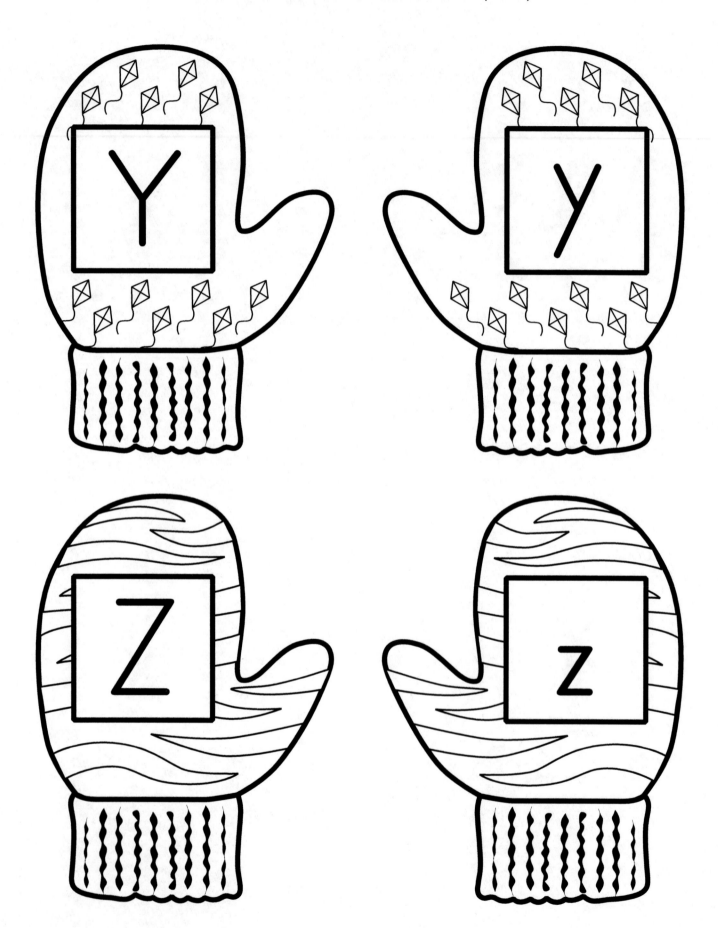

Alphabet Snake

Uppercase

Teacher Directions: Use the Alphabet Snake pages to help your children learn alphabetical order with both upper- and lowercase letters. Reproduce pages 181–184 and have the students cut out the lettered snake parts. Let them glue the snake parts together alphabetically, from end to end, in a wavy snake-like fashion. Tape one end of a length of yarn to the head of each snake so the children can pull their snakes across a tabletop to resemble actual movement.

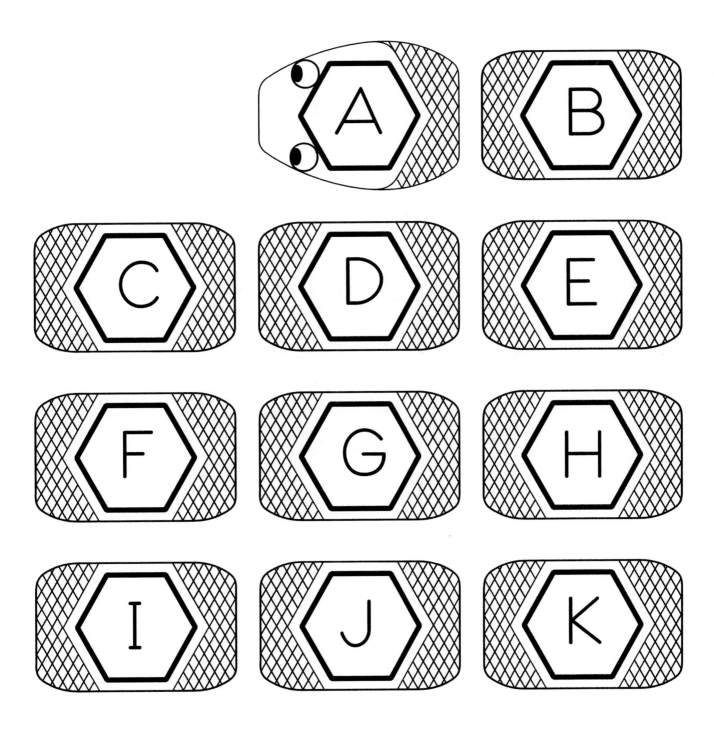

Uppercase

Alphabet Snake (cont.)

Lowercase

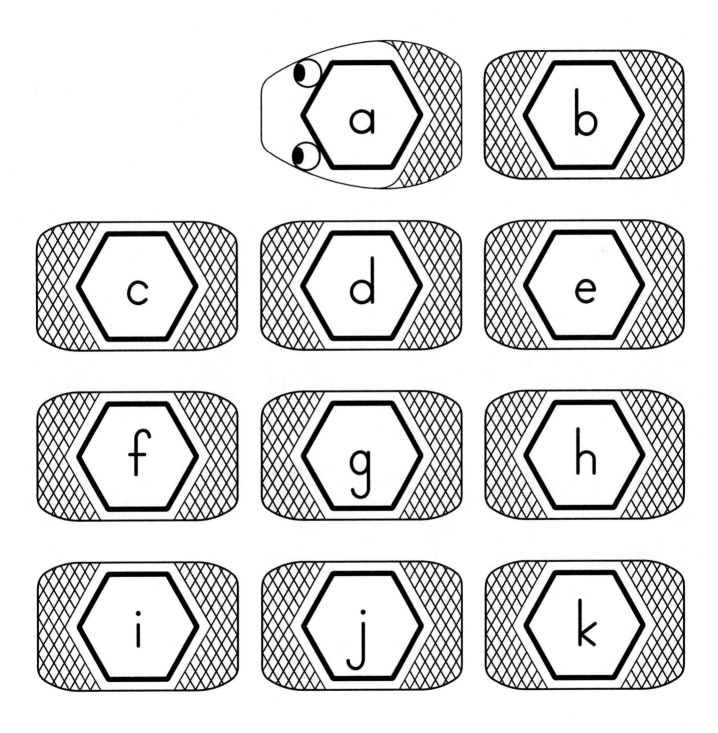

Alphabet Snake *(cont.)*

Lowercase

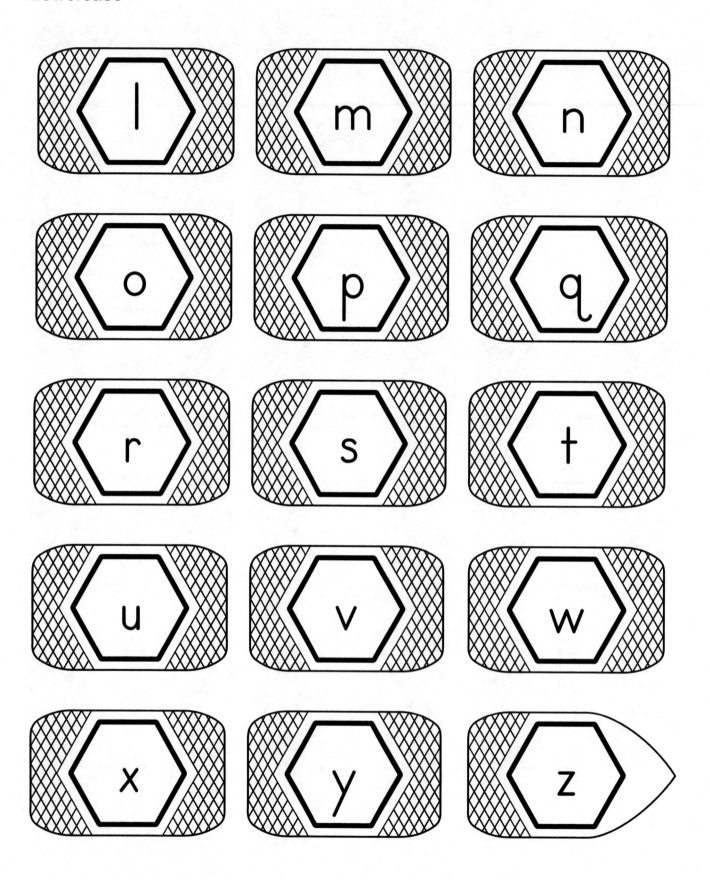

Color Name Cards

Teacher Directions: Reproduce this as a double-sided page with page 186 and have the children cut the cards apart. Use the cards with the class to help the students learn to recognize color name words, and let the children work in pairs to practice. You can also reproduce a set of cards for each child to take home for practice.

red	blue
yellow	green
orange	purple
brown	black

Color Name Cards

Teacher Directions: Reproduce this as a double-sided page with page 185 and use as directed on page 185. Complete each card by coloring these circles to match the corresponding color word on the back of each card.

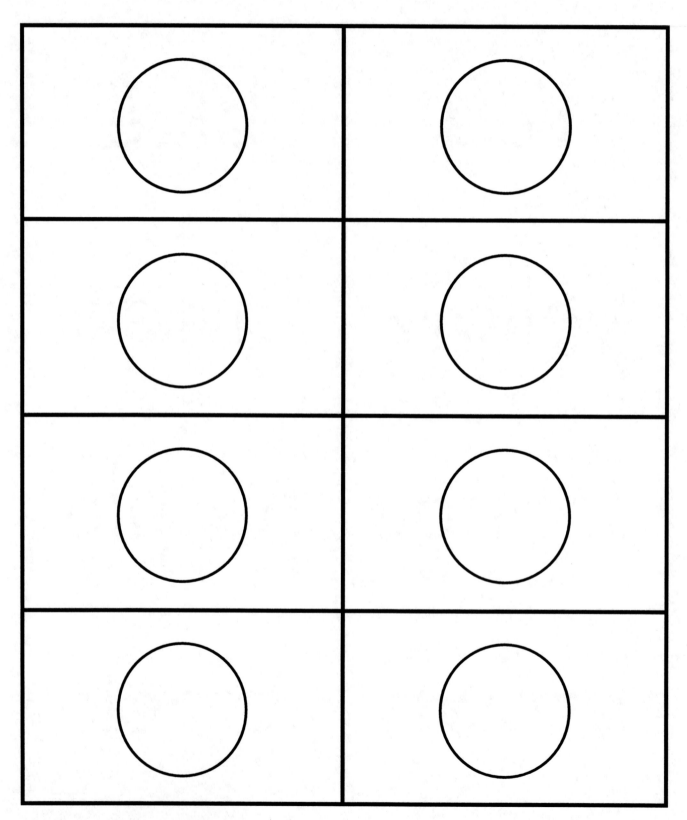

Number Name Cards

Teacher Directions: Reproduce pages 187–190 and have the students cut the cards apart. Suggested uses for these cards:

1. Use these cards with the Number Names math activity on page 12.
2. Shuffle the cards. Challenge the children to match number and number name cards; number cards with groups of objects; number name cards with groups of objects.
3. Use as flashcards.

0	zero
1	one

Number Name Cards *(cont.)*

2	two
3	three
4	four

Number Name Cards *(cont.)*

5	five
6	six
7	seven

Number Name Cards *(cont.)*

8	eight
q	nine
10	ten

Poster Book

Invite the children to work as a team to create a letter sound big book. Place the finished product in your classroom library for independent browsing.

Materials: 26 large sheets of construction paper, crayons and/or markers, metal key rings from a hardware or craft store, one or more of your favorite ABC books

Directions:

1. Share one or more of your favorite ABC books with the class. Talk about letter names and sounds.

2. Assign the children, or have them choose, one letter each. Have them write both upper- and lowercase forms of their letters at the top of large sheets of construction paper.

3. Help them each choose one object their letter will represent. Have them draw and color a picture of this object below the letter forms.

4. Invite them to dictate a caption for you to write on each page. Let them sign their work.

5. Punch three or four holes down the left side of each page. Have the children work to place the pages in alphabetical order. Bind the book with metal rings and then place it in your classroom library.

Additional Uses:

1. Display the pages, in alphabetical order, on a bulletin board before binding them into a book.

2. Display the book at Open House for the parents to enjoy.

Junior Journal

Student journals demonstrate how reading and writing are integrated, while allowing children to progress at their own rate. Journals help students visualize how letters are used to form words and words combine to create sentences. Early entries will be mainly pictorial, captioned with words dictated to the teacher. The children will gradually begin to copy or "spell" their own words.

Invite your students to glue stickers or colorful paper shapes to the front of composition books to create covers for their journals. Be sure to set aside a time in your daily schedule for making journal entries, and have the children date each entry.

Journal Topic Ideas

1. Help the children write their address at the top of the page. Have them draw pictures of their home below.

2. Let the children draw pictures of what they had for breakfast this morning. Help them label each food.

3. Have the children draw pictures of how they got to school today. Did they walk, take a bus, ride a bike, or arrive by car? Help them caption their drawings with simple sentences.

4. Have the children draw pictures of something they like/dislike to do. Help them caption their drawings with descriptions of why they like/dislike this action.

5. Let them draw pictures of their best friends. Write the person's name and what makes this person a best friend.

6. Help the children write titles of favorite stories at the top of the page. Draw pictures of the best part of the stories below.

7. Have them draw pictures of a dream they had, then dictate the dream for you to write.

8. Let them write Pet Shop at the top of the page. Draw pictures of pets they would like to have below. Label the animals with correct names.

9. Help them write the titles of their favorite songs at the top of the page. Draw a picture about the song below.

10. Have the children draw something silly, scary, sad, long, short, hot, cold, etc. Then write or dictate a description of their drawings.

Finish the Letters

Fill in the missing pieces to make the letters in each box match.

A ∧	O C
S ᔕ	M ∧
K ∧	D ⊃
E ⊏	H ‖
T ⊤	Z ≡

Mystery Page

Fill in the missing letters.

Start here →

			B
C		E	F
	H		J
	L	M	
O		Q	
S	T		V
	X		Z

Mystery Page *(cont.)*

Fill in the missing letters.

Start here →

	a	
c	d		f
	h	i	
k		m	
o	p		r
	t		v
w			z

Letter Graph

Materials: graph page for each child, tray of alphabet-shaped cereal or pasta, glue, and pencils (Craft note: You may be able to obtain colorful alphabet pasta from a school supply catalog or at your local craft store.)

Teacher Directions:

Invite your students to sort through the alphabet-shaped cereal or pasta to find letters for their graph. Then, have them glue the items in the appropriate column to match letters. Have them count the number of glued letters in each column and write the totals in the boxes below.

Safety Note: Tell the children that this collage material is not for eating. Supervise the activity. Set aside additional cereal or pasta to share for snack at a later time, if you wish.

A	B	C	D	E	F	G	H	I

Letter Graph *(cont.)*

J	K	L	M	N	O	P	Q	R

Letter Graph *(cont.)*

S	T	U	V	W	X	Y	Z	name

Letter Match

Uppercase

Directions: Circle the letters that match in each row.

A	L A M A W A
H	K L H Y H Z T
P	B P D C P O L
W	W N X W Z W
G	O G D G G B
K	K N K L M K I

Letter Match *(cont.)*

Lowercase

Directions: Circle the letters that match in each row.

d	a d b c d p
f	f k l f h f i
e	g e a o e c
p	d p b p a p
r	r m r n a r
h	m h k h b d

Letter Match *(cont.)*

Upper- to Lowercase

Directions: Circle the letters that match in each row.

M	M Z N M Y E N
y	z y k y y x i z
Q	O C Q D S Q C
a	a b q a c d q
Z	K Z W Z M Z
n	n a n r m n

Hidden Pictures

The Birthday Party

Directions: Allie's friends all brought capital letter gifts to the party. They hid them throughout the room. Help Allie find her gifts. Circle the letters you find.

Hidden Pictures *(cont.)*

The Messy Room

Teacher Directions: Jason spilled his box of lower case letters in his messy room. Help Jason find his lower case letters. Circle the ones you find.

Fall Sounds

Directions: Color the pictures of the sounds that match. Circle one fall picture in each row.

Winter Sounds

Directions: Color the pictures of the sounds that match. Circle one winter picture in each row.

Spring Sounds

Directions: Color the pictures of the sounds that match. Circle one spring picture in each row.

Summer Sounds

Directions: Color the pictures of the sounds that match. Circle one summer picture in each row.

Crayon Cut-outs

Teacher Directions:

1. Make a copy of the crayons for each child. Help the children read the color names. Have them color the crayons appropriately, then cut the crayons out.

2. Make a color hat. Provide each child with a hat-size paper strip. Have the children glue the crayons vertically across the paper strip. Size the bands to the children's heads, then staple in place.

3. Make a color mobile. Help the children cut a length of yarn for each of their Crayon Cut-outs. Tape one end of each yarn piece to one end of each cut-out. Tape the opposite end of each yarn length to a clothes hanger to make a mobile for each student.

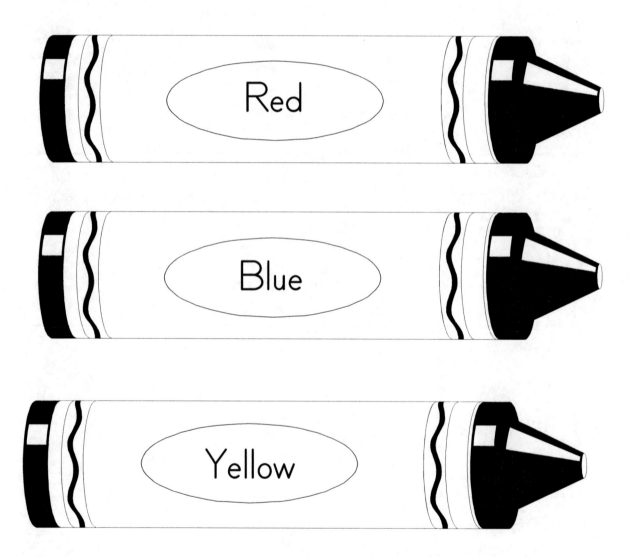

Crayon Cut-outs *(cont.)*

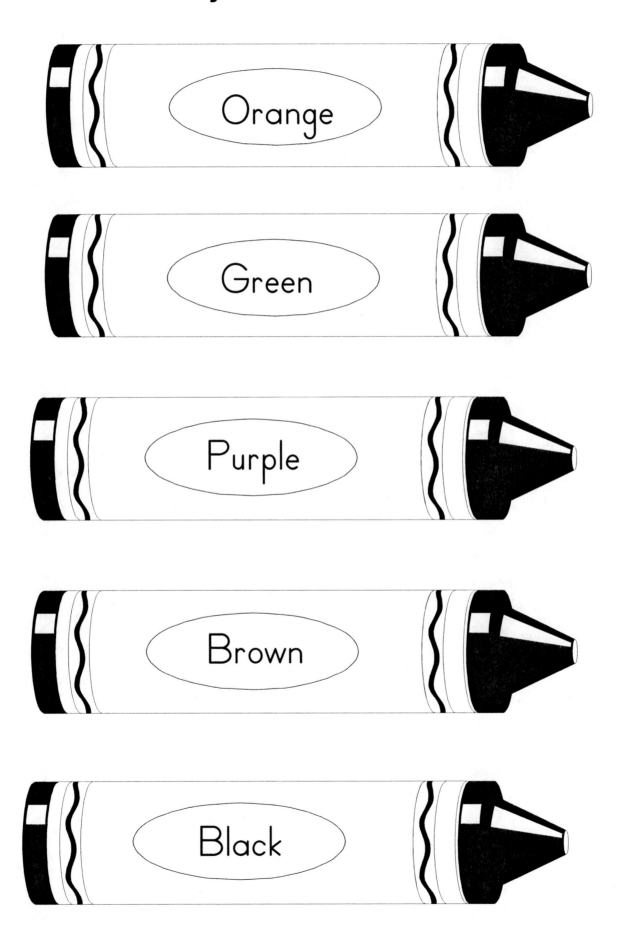

Orange

Green

Purple

Brown

Black

Clothesline Colors

Directions: Color the shirts. Cut out the shirts at the right. Glue them on the correct clothesline.

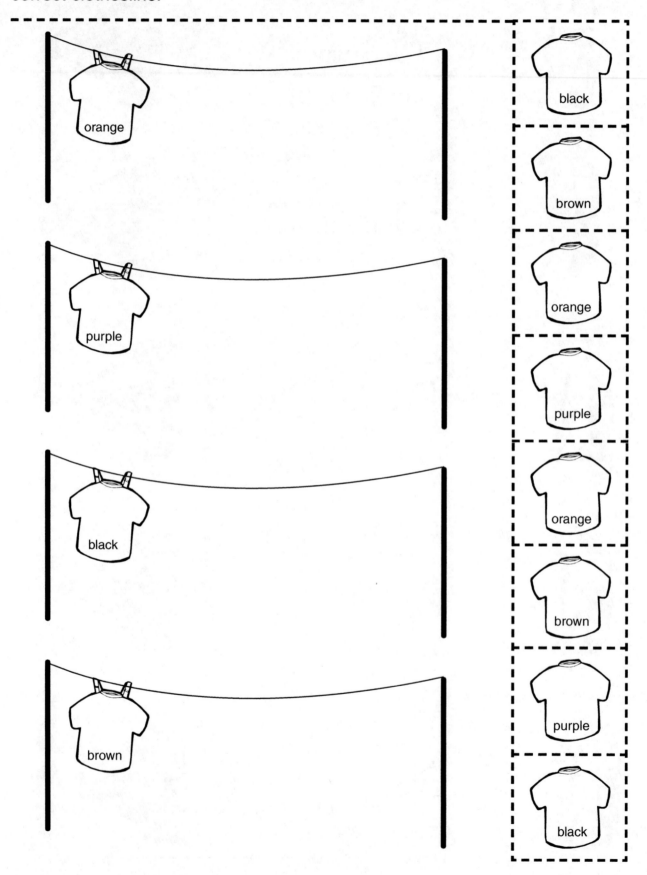

Birthday Balloons

Directions: Color all the balloons. Cut out the balloons at the bottom. Glue them on top of their same colors in the picture above.

Award Medallions

Teacher Directions: As individual students master the letter names and their sounds, acknowledge their progress by presenting each with an Award Medallion. Cut out each award and write the student's name on the line, then glue the award to a cardboard circle. Punch a hole at the top of the award. Thread ribbon through the hole and knot the ends of the ribbon together to create a medallion necklace.

Letter Master

_____

Sound Master

_____

Dear Parents,

Throughout the year, students will be participating in many alphabet-related activities. They will learn the names of individual letters and the sounds these letters represent; they will come to understand that when these sounds are blended together, words are formed. Learning letter sounds will also help the children begin to write their own words. Learning letters and sounds means we are learning to read and write.

We need to incorporate reading and writing into each child's everyday experiences so they may experience these activities in meaningful ways. We need to make use of the child's speaking vocabulary and personal experiences to demonstrate that we read and write for a purpose. Below are suggestions for activities you can do at home:

1. Read to your child. This is one of the most important readiness activities you can do together. Make sure your child receives a library card, and use it on a regular basis.

2. Help your child to notice words around the house, such as those found on can labels, boxes, bottles, jars, and food wrappers. Work with your child to label other items such as a desk, lamp, book, table, door, etc.

3. Help your child become aware of printed words around town, such as those found on road signs and stores, or at the movies. At home, work together to build a box village. Label your buildings.

4. Have your child help make the grocery shopping list and sort out the coupons you will need.

5. Find the date on the calendar each day. Share the names of the days of the week and months of the year.

6. Work on cooking projects together. Read the recipes.

7. Go out to eat. Read the menu.

8. Make a "to do" list together, for a day, weekend, a special trip, or a party.

9. Plant a garden together. Read the seed packets.

10. Help your child write thank you notes for all gifts received.

11. Help your child create a homemade book collection. Let the child illustrate the pages and dictate words for you to write. Encourage your child to read the book(s) to others.

Enjoy the time you share with your child.

Sincerely,

A Whale of a Tale

Parents: Let your child connect the dots alphabetically to create a whale. Color it blue. Help your child write a short story about the whale on a separate sheet of paper. Please return both pages to school to share with the class.

Dancing Dinosaur Puppet

Parents: Let your child connect the dots alphabetically to create a dinosaur. Color it green, cut it out, and then tape it to a craft stick or a strip of cardboard to make a stick puppet. Have your child make the dinosaur dance while you sing the alphabet song together.

Alphabet Pocket Pack

Teacher Directions:

1. Have the children trace the letters, then cut the cards apart.

2. Provide the students with letter-sized envelopes. Let them write their names on the front of the envelopes, then place their cards inside.

3. Include a copy of the At Home Game Ideas below in each envelope.

4. Encourage the children to share their personal card packs and game ideas with their families.

At-Home Game Ideas:

1. Use as flashcards to practice letter names.

2. Use as flashcards to practice letter sounds.

3. Match letters with objects around the home for initial sounds.

4. Mix the cards up, then have your child place them in alphabetical order.

5. Lay the cards out, faceup, on a tabletop. Call out the names or sounds of individual letters for your child to pick up.

6. Hide the cards throughout one room of the house. Give your child one minute to search the room and retrieve cards. Work together to place the retrieved cards in alphabetical order. Which letters are you missing?

7. Ask your child for example: How many letters are in the alphabet? How can we find out? (Hint: Count the cards!)

8. Ask the whole family to put on their thinking caps. In what other ways might these cards be used? Invent games of your own.

Alphabet Pocket Pack Cards

A a	B b
C c	D d
E e	F f
G g	H h
I i	J j

Alphabet Pocket Pack Cards *(cont.)*

K k	L l
M m	N n
O o	P p
Q q	R r
S s	T t

Alphabet Pocket Pack Cards *(cont.)*

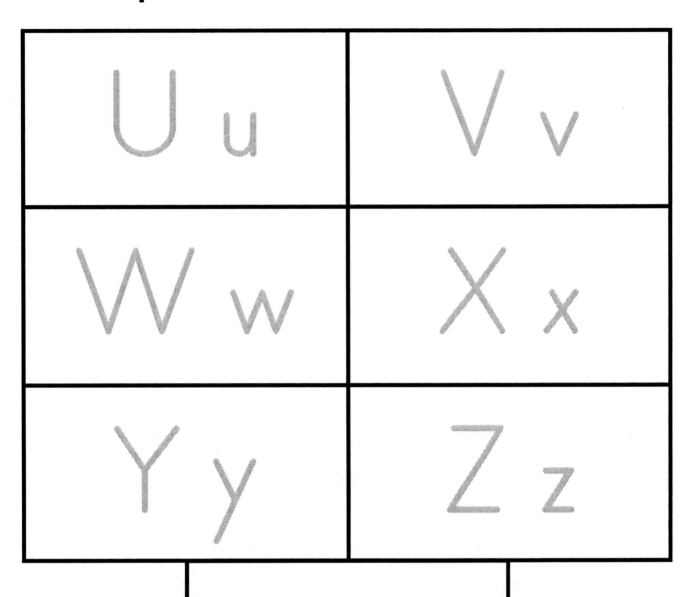

Color Word Puzzles

Teacher Directions: Cut out the individual puzzles and send each home with a copy of the letter below as your class works to recognize color names.

Dear Parents,

We are learning to recognize color names at school. In the upcoming weeks, your child will be bringing home color name puzzles to make and use at home to reinforce our schoolwork. Please help your child to read the color words, cut the puzzle pieces apart, then work to put the words back together. Store each puzzle in an envelope so your child can practice these words.

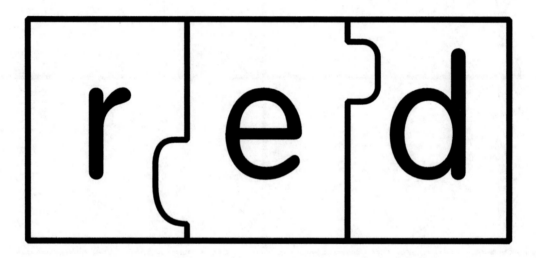

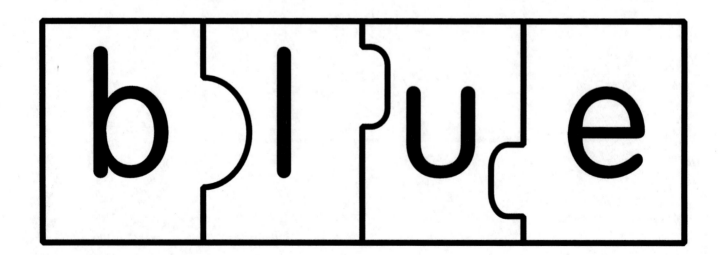

Color Word Puzzles *(cont.)*

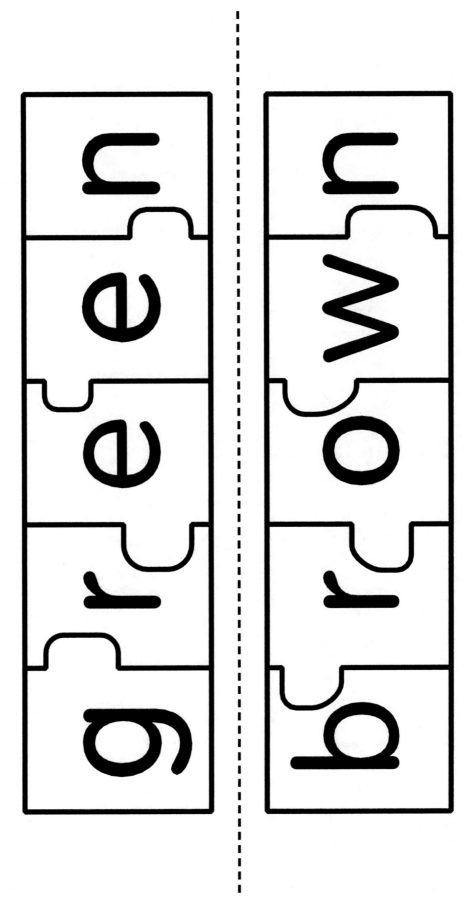

Color Word Puzzles _(cont.)_

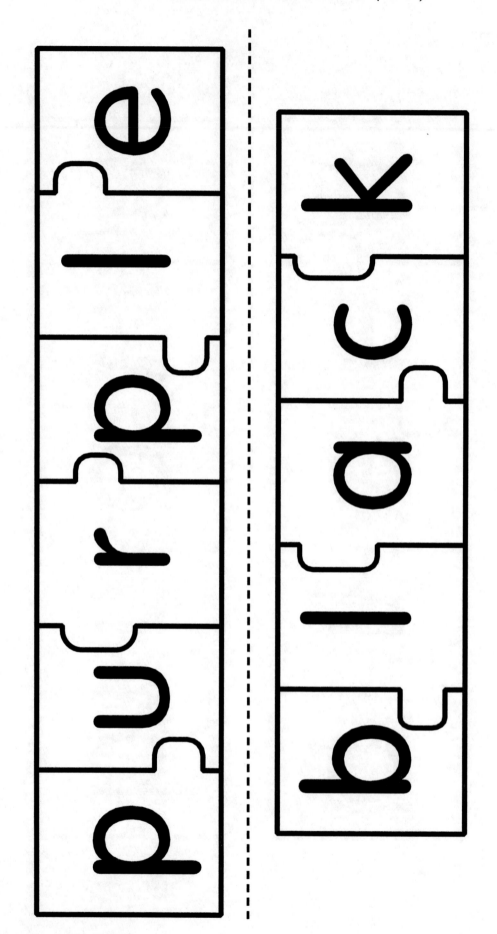

Color Word Puzzles *(cont.)*

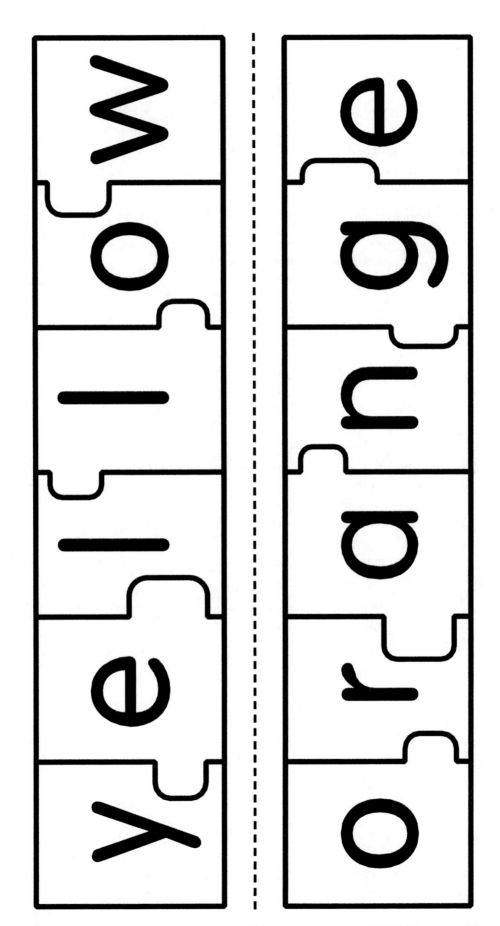

Bibliography

Books

Baker, Alan. *Black and White Rabbits ABC*. Scholastic, 1994.

Baynton, Sandra. *A to Z*. Simon & Schuster, 1995.

Bender Robert. *A to Z Beastly Jamboree*. Lodestar, 1996.

Carter, David. *Alpha Bugs*. Scholastic, 1994.

Dodson, Peter. *An Alphabet of Dinosaurs*. Syron Press Visual Publishing, 1995.

Drucker, Malka. *A Jewish Holiday ABC*. Trumpet, 1996.

Fain, Kathleen. *Handsigns*. Scholastic, 1993.

Geddes, Anne. *ABC*. Cedco Publishing Co., 1995.

Hague, Kathleen. *Alphabears: An ABC Book*. Henry Holt, 1991.

Hirashima, Jean. *ABC*. Random House, 1994.

Hofbauer, Michele Pace. *All the Letters*. Green Bark Press, 1993.

Jordan, Martin and Tanis. *Amazon Alphabet*. Kingfisher, 1996.

Lionni, Leo. *The Alphabet Tree*. Trumpet Club, 1990.

Murphy, Chuck. *My First Book of the Alphabet*. Scholastic, 1993. Charlesbridge, 1996.

Pallotta, Jerry. *The Underwater Alphabet Book*. Charlesbridge, 1991.

The Icky Bug Alphabet Book. Charlesbridge, 1990.

The Yucky Reptile Alphabet Book. Charlesbridge, 1990.

Pelletier, David. *The Graphic Alphabet*. Orchard, 1996.

Peterson, Roger Tory. *ABC of Birds*. Universe Publishing, 1995.

Ryden, Hope. *The ABC or Crawlers and Flyers*. Clarion, 1996.

Sardegna, Jill. *K Is for Kiss Good Night*: *A Bedtime Alphabet*. Bantam, Doubleday, Dell Publishing, 1996.

Schories, Pat. *Over Under in the Garden*. Farrar, Straus, & Giroux Inc., 1996.

Seuss, Dr. *Dr. Seuss's ABC*. Random House, 1996.

Shannon, George. *Tomorrow's Alphabet*. Greenwillow, 1996.

Tapahonso, Lucy. *Navajo ABC: A Dine Alphabet Book*. Simon & Schuster, 1995.

Wilbur, Richard. *The Disappearing Alphabet*. Harcourt, Brace & Company, 1997.

Wood, Jerry. *Animal Parade*. Scholastic, 1993.

Technology: VHS

Alphabet Soup. Videotape. Warner Studios, 1995. 30 minutes.

Sesame Street—The Jungle Game. Videotape. Sony Wonder Studios, 1998. 28 minutes.

Technology: CD

JumpStart Reading for Kindergartners. CD-ROM. Knowledge Adventure. 1311 Grand Central Avenue, Glendale, CA 91201. (818) 246-4400.

Land Before Time Animated Preschool Adventure. CD. MacMillan/McGraw-Hill. 1221 Avenue of the Americas, New York, NY 10020.

Leap Ahead! Preschool. CD. Mattel Interactive. 1 Martha's Way, Hiawatha, IA 52233. (319) 395-9626.

Leap Ahead! Phonics. CD. Mattel Interactive. 1 Martha's Way, Hiawatha, IA 52233. (319) 395-9626.

Reader Rabbit's Complete Learn to Read System. CD. Mattel Interactive. 1 Martha's Way, Hiawatha, IA 52233. (319) 395-9626.

Sesame Street: Elmo's Reading-Preschool and K. Mattel Interactive. CD. Mattel Interactive. 1 Martha's Way, Hiawatha, IA 52233. (319) 395-9626.